The Easy Piano Hymn Collection

TABLE OF CONTENTS

2 Abide with Me	56 Jesus Loves Me
4 All Glory, Laud and Honor	58 Just As I Am
6 All Hail the Power of Jesus' Name	55 Lead On, O King Eternal
9 Amazing Grace	62 Leaning on the Everlasting Arms
12 At Calvary	64 Let Us Break Bread Together
14 At the Cross	70 A Mighty Fortress Is Our God
16 Blest Be the Tie That Binds	72 Nearer, My God, to Thee
18 Christ the Lord Is Risen Today	67 Now Thank We All Our God
20 Church in the Wildwood	74 O for a Thousand Tongues to Sing
22 The Church's One Foundation	75 O God, Our Help in Ages Past
23 Come, Christians, Join to Sing	76 The Old Rugged Cross
26 Crown Him with Many Crowns	82 Onward, Christian Soldiers
28 Fairest Lord Jesus	79 Open My Eyes, That I May See
30 Faith of Our Fathers	84 Praise God, from Whom All Blessings Flow
32 For All the Saints	86 Praise to the Lord, the Almighty
34 For the Beauty of the Earth	88 Precious Memories
36 God of Grace and God of Glory	90 Rock of Ages
38 God of Our Fathers	92 Softly and Tenderly
29 He Leadeth Me	96 Sweet By and By
40 Heavenly Sunlight	95 Sweet Hour of Prayer
46 Higher Ground	98 Take My Life and Let It Be
43 Holy God, We Praise Thy Name	99 We Gather Together
48 Holy, Holy, Holy	100 What a Friend We Have in Jesus
50 I Love to Tell the Story	104 When I Survey the Wondrous Cross
54 I Need Thee Every Hour	102 When We All Get to Heaven

ISBN 978-0-634-02919-6

HAL•LEONARD®
CORPORATION

7777 W. BLUEMOUND RD. P.O. BOX 13819 MILWAUKEE, WI 53213

Visit Hal Leonard Online at
www.halleonard.com

ABIDE WITH ME

Words by HENRY F. LYTE
Music by WILLIAM H. MONK

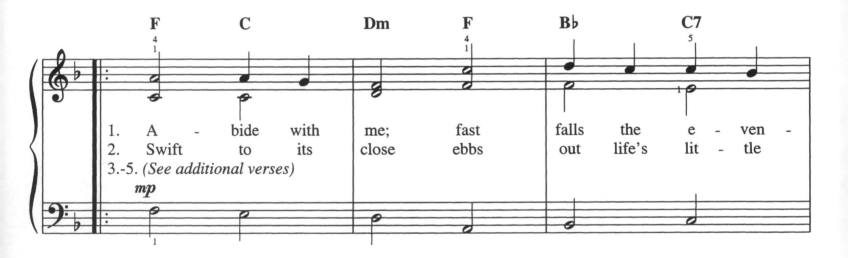

1. A - bide with me; fast falls the e - ven -
2. Swift to its close fast ebbs out life's lit - tle
3.-5. *(See additional verses)*

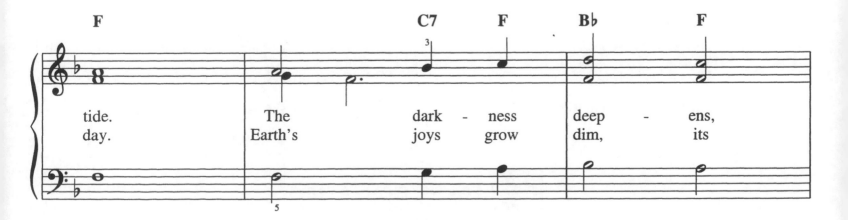

tide. The dark - ness deep - ens,
day. Earth's joys grow dim, its

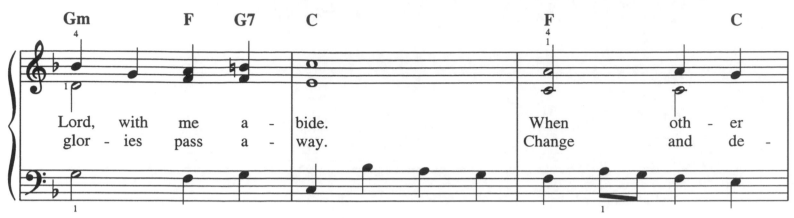

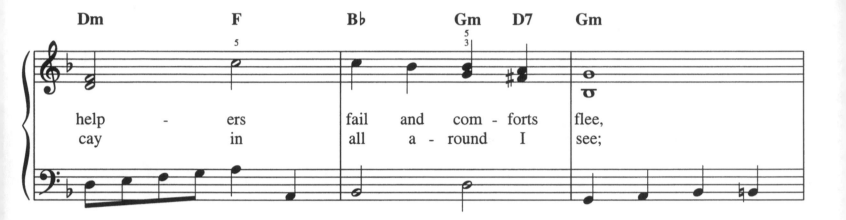

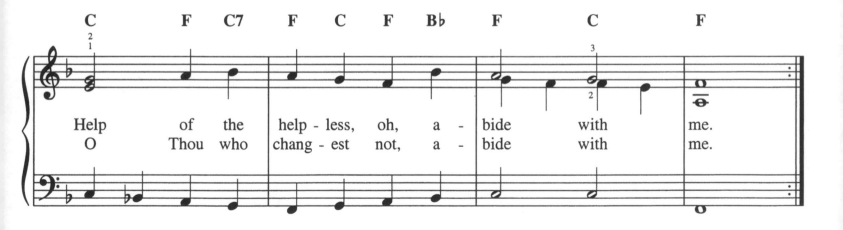

Additional Verses

3. I need thy presence every passing hour.
   What but thy grace can foil the tempter's power?
   Who, like thyself, my guide and stay can be?
   Through cloud and sunshine, Lord, abide with me.

4. I fear no foe, with thee at hand to bless;
   ills have no weight, and tears no bitterness.
   Where is death's sting? Where, grave, thy victory?
   I triumph still, if thou abide with me.

5. Hold thou thy cross before my closing eyes;
   shine through the gloom and point me to the skies.
   Heaven's morning breaks, and earth's vain shadows flee;
   in life, in death, O Lord, abide with me.

ALL GLORY, LAUD AND HONOR

Words by THEODULPH OF ORLEANS
Translated by JOHN MASON NEALE
Music by MELCHIOR TESCHNER

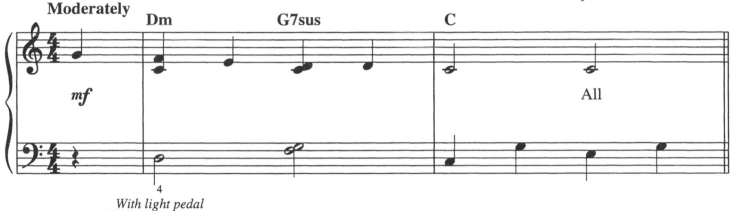

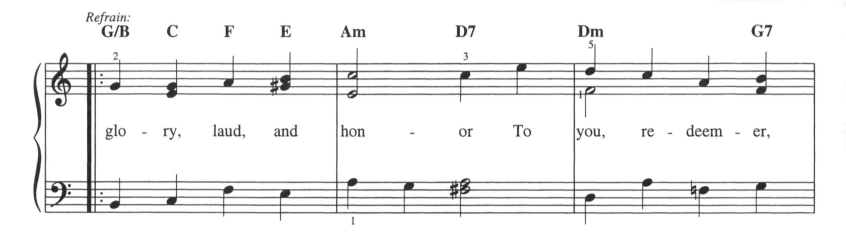

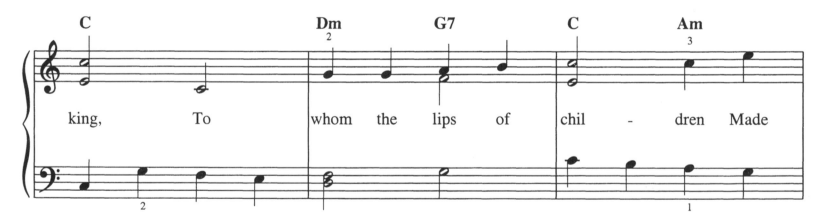

Additional Verses

3. The multitude of pilgrims
   With palms before you went.
   Our praise and prayer and anthems
   Before you we present.
   Refrain:

4. To you, before your Passion,
   They sang their hymns of praise.
   To you, now high exalted,
   Our melody we raise.

ALL HAIL THE POWER
OF JESUS' NAME

Words by EDWARD PERRONET
Altered by JOHN RIPPON
Music by OLIVER HOLDEN

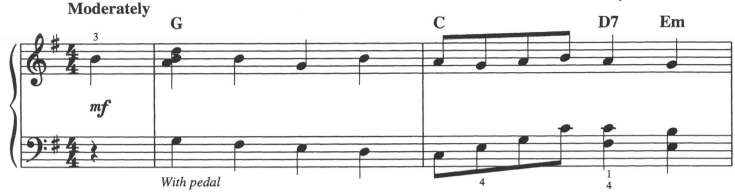

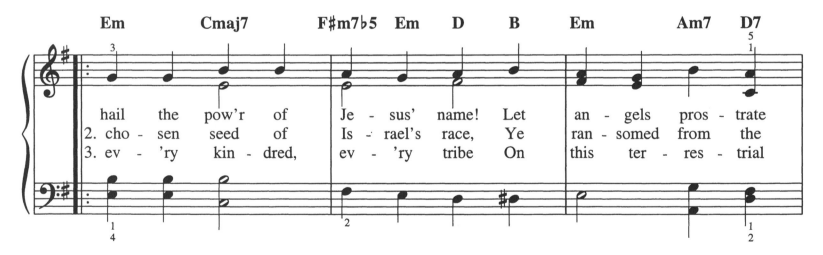

hail the pow'r of Je - sus' name! Let an - gels pros - trate
2. cho - sen seed of Is - rael's race, Ye ran - somed from the
3. ev - 'ry kin - dred, ev - 'ry tribe On this ter - res - trial

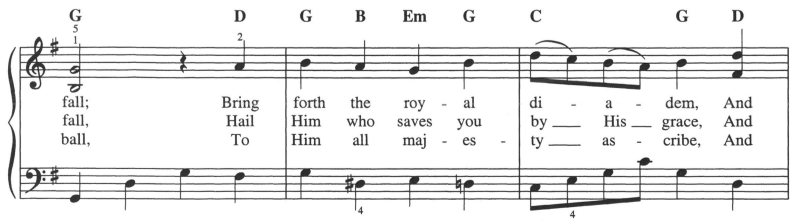

fall; Bring forth the roy - al di - a - dem, And
fall, Hail Him who saves you by ___ His ___ grace, And
ball, To Him all maj - es - ty ___ as - cribe, And

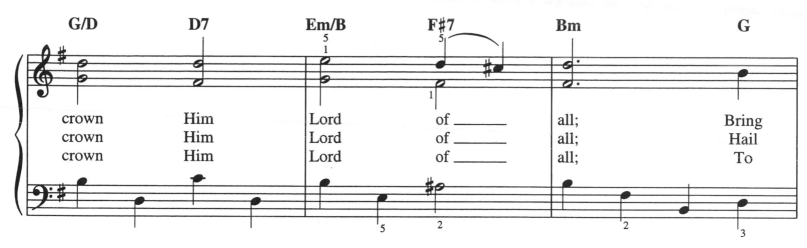

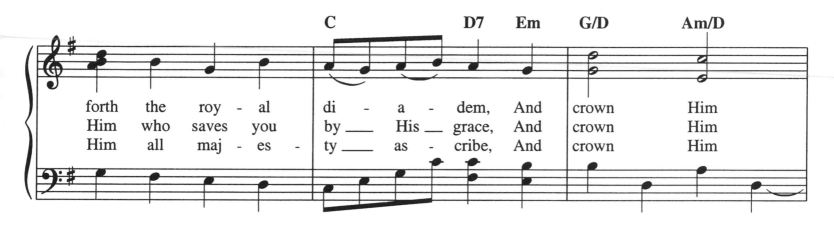

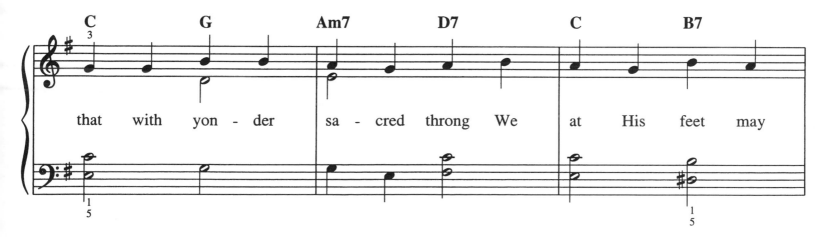

8

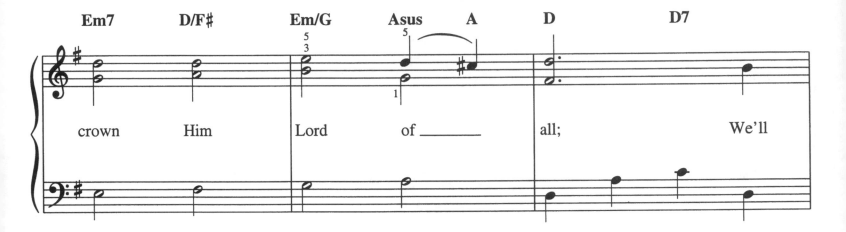

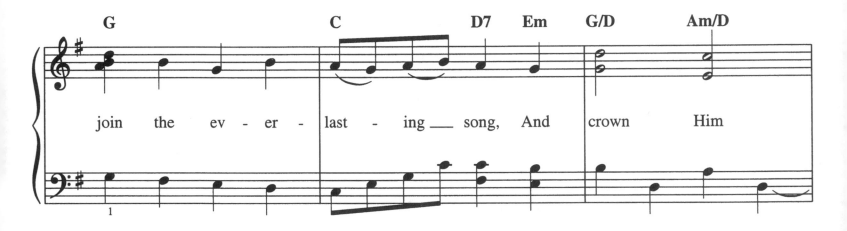

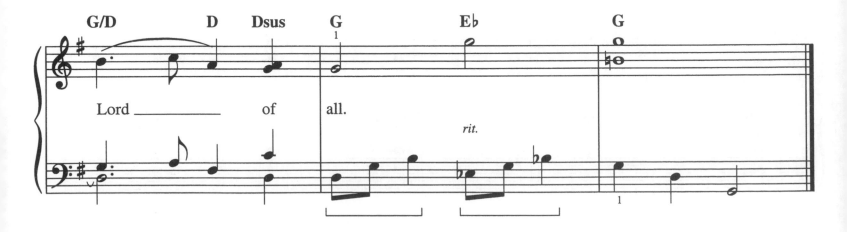

AMAZING GRACE

Words by JOHN NEWTON
Traditional American Melody

Slowly, with reverence

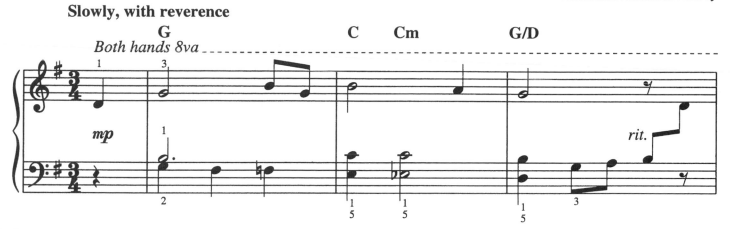

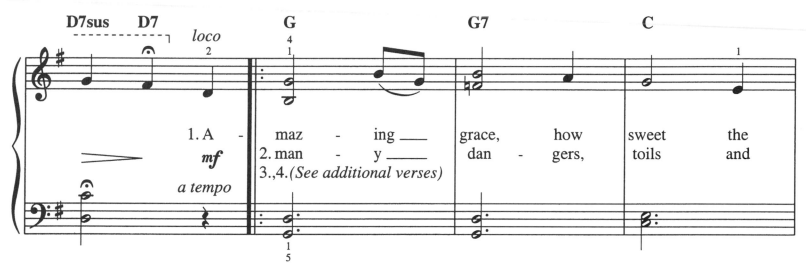

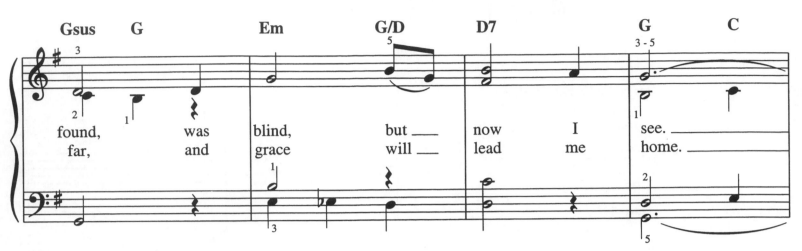

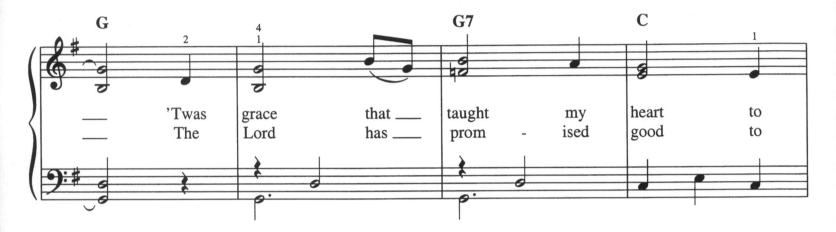

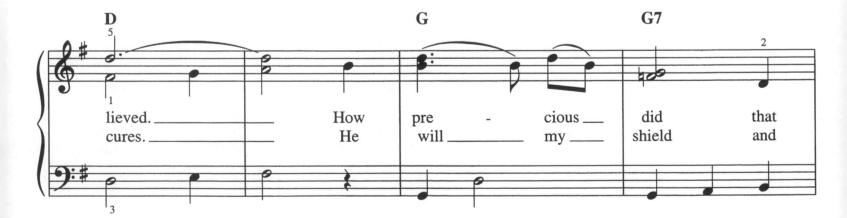

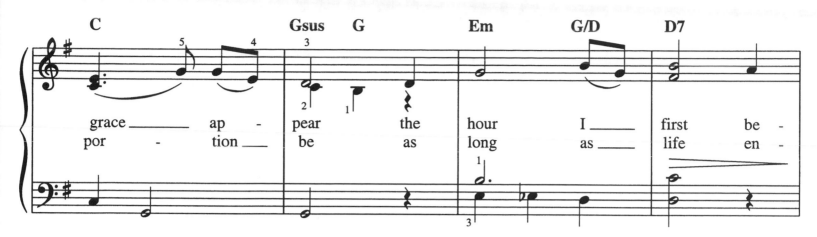

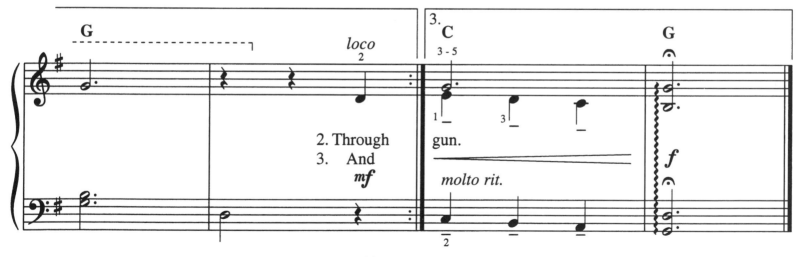

Additional Verses

3. And when this flesh and heart shall fail
   And mortal life shall cease,
   I shall possess within the veil
   A life of joy and peace.

4. When we've been there ten thousand years,
   Bright shining as the sun,
   We've no less days to sing God's praise
   Than when we first begun.

AT CALVARY

Words by WILLIAM R. NEWELL
Music by DANIEL B. TOWNER

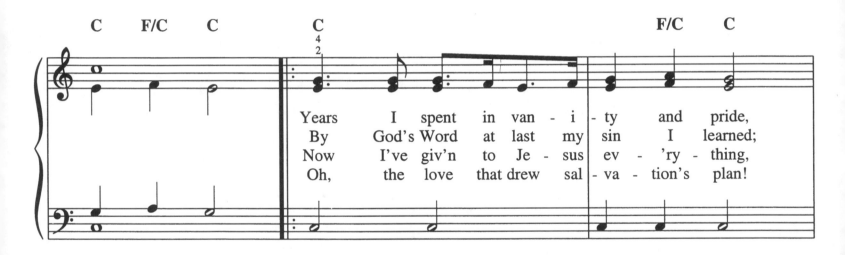

Years I spent in van - i - ty and pride,
By God's Word at last my sin I learned;
Now I've giv'n to Je - sus ev - 'ry - thing,
Oh, the love that drew sal - va - tion's plan!

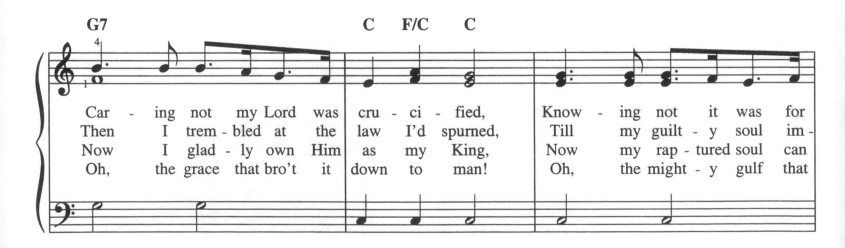

Car - ing not my Lord was cru - ci - fied, Know - ing not it was for
Then I trem - bled at the law I'd spurned, Till my guilt - y soul im -
Now I glad - ly own Him as my King, Now my rap - tured soul can
Oh, the grace that bro't it down to man! Oh, the might - y gulf that

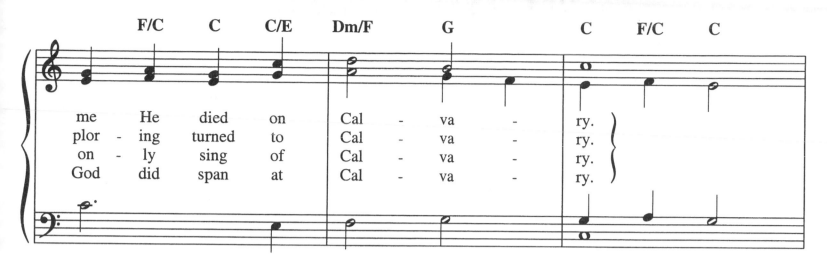

me He died on Cal - va - ry.
plor - ing turned to Cal - va - ry.
on - ly sing of Cal - va - ry.
God did span at Cal - va - ry.

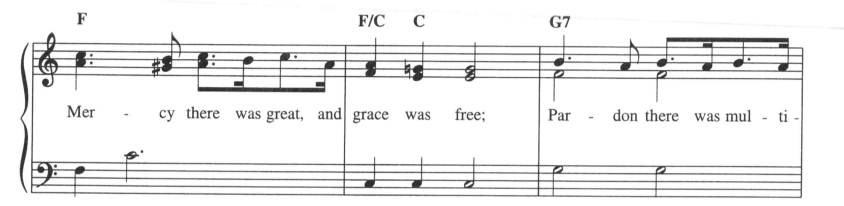

Mer - cy there was great, and grace was free; Par - don there was mul - ti -

plied to me; There my bur - dened soul found lib - er - ty At

Cal - va - ry.
ry.

AT THE CROSS

Words by ISAAC WATTS and RALPH E. HUDSON
Music by RALPH E. HUDSON

Moderately

With light pedal

1. A - las, and did my
2. it for crimes that
3.,4. *(See additional verses)*

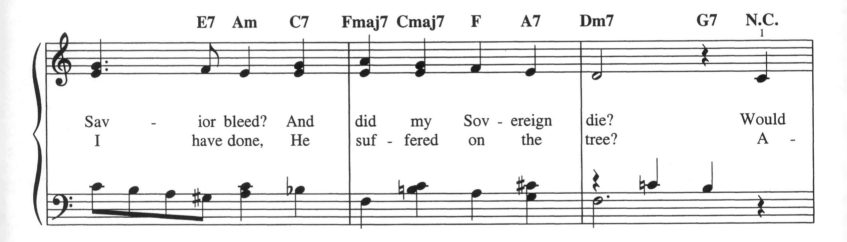

Sav - ior bleed? And did my Sov - ereign die? Would
I have done, He suf - fered on the tree? A -

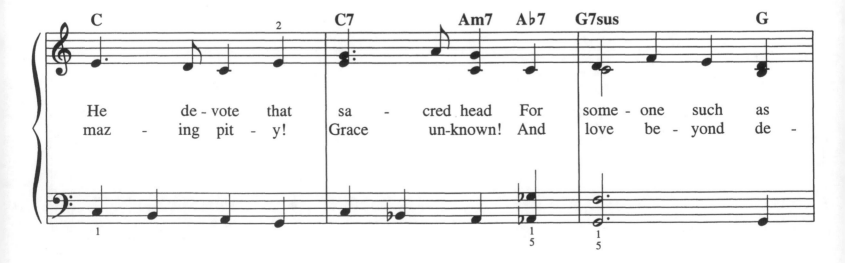

He de - vote that sa - cred head For some - one such as
maz - ing pit - y! Grace un-known! And love be - yond de -

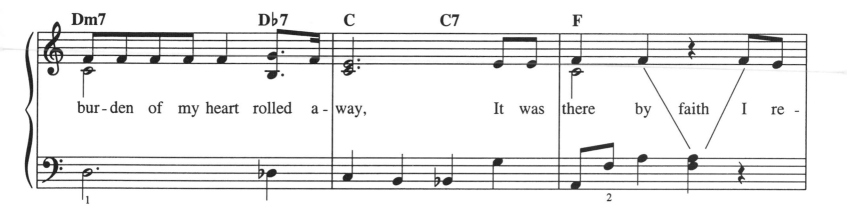

Additional Verses

3. Well might the sun in darkness hide
   And shut his glories in,
   When Christ, the mighty Maker, died
   For man the creature's sin.
   Refrain:

4. But drops of grief can ne'er repay
   The debt of love I owe;
   Here, Lord, I give myself away,
   'Tis all that I can do!
   Refrain:

15

BLEST BE THE TIE THAT BINDS

Words by JOHN FAWCETT
Music by JOHANN G. NÄGELI
Arranged by LOWELL MASON

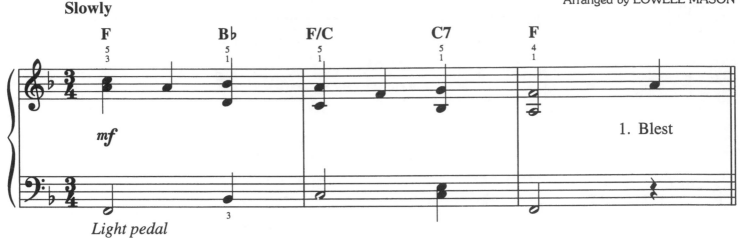

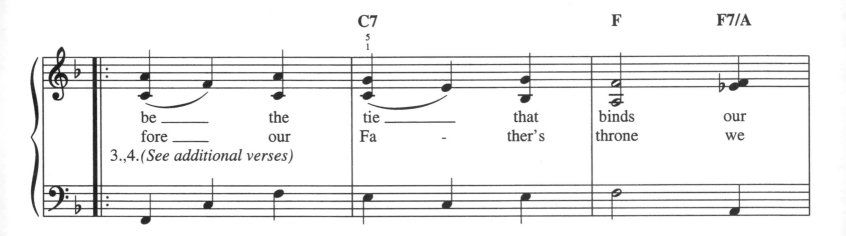

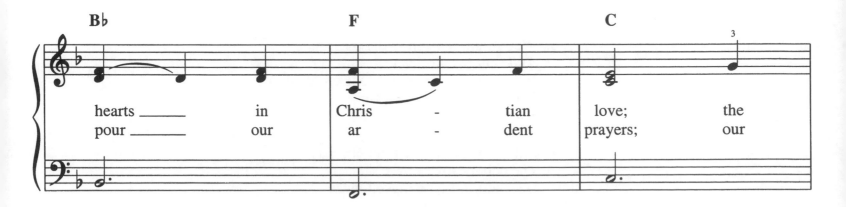

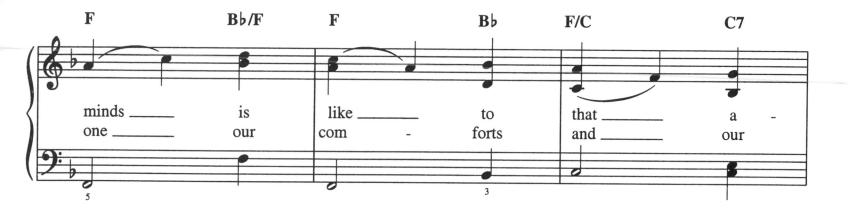

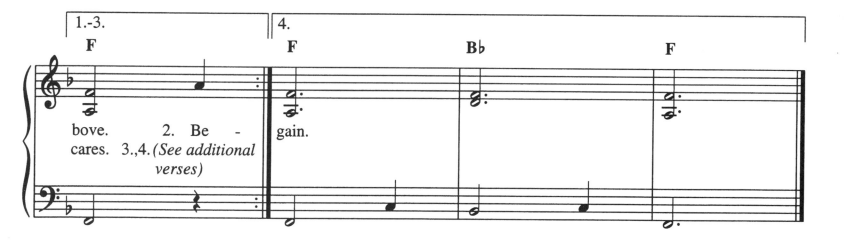

Additional Verses

3. We share each other's woes,
   Our mutual burdens bear;
   And often for each other flows
   The sympathizing tear.

4. When we asunder part,
   It gives us inward pain;
   But we shall still be joined in heart,
   And hope to meet again.

CHRIST THE LORD IS RISEN TODAY

Words by CHARLES WESLEY
Music adapted from *Lyra Davidica*

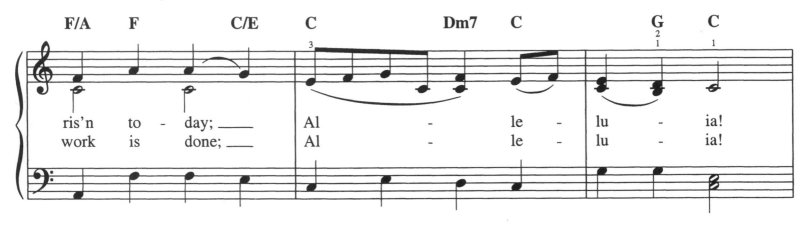

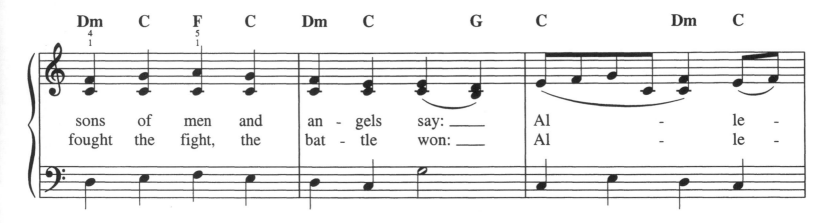

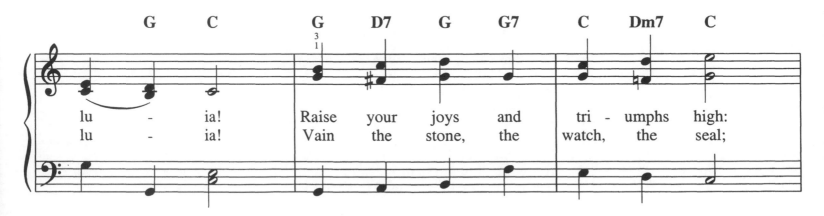

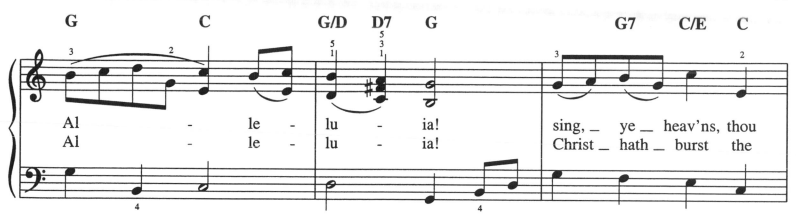

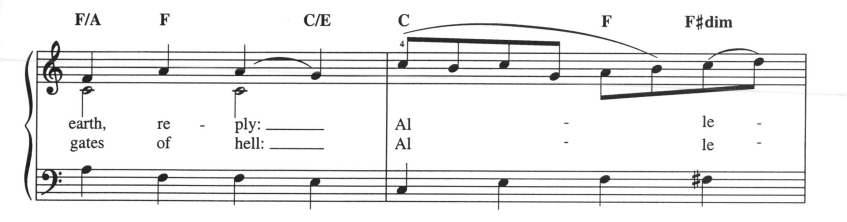

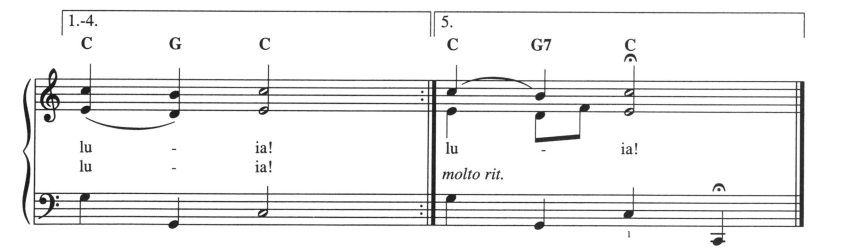

Additional Verses

3. Lives again our glorious King; Alleluia,
   where, O death, is now thy sting? Alleluia.
   Once he died our souls to save; Alleluia,
   where's thy victory, boasting grave? Alleluia.

4. Soar we now where Christ hath led, Alleluia,
   following our exalted head: Alleluia.
   Made like him, like him we rise; Alleluia,
   ours the cross, the grave, the skies: Alleluia.

5. King of glory! Soul of bliss! Alleluia,
   Everlasting life is this, Alleluia.
   Thee to know, thy power to prove, Alluluia,
   thus to sing, and thus to love: Alleluia.

CHURCH IN THE WILDWOOD

Words and Music by
DR. WILLIAM S. PITTS

Moderate steady beat

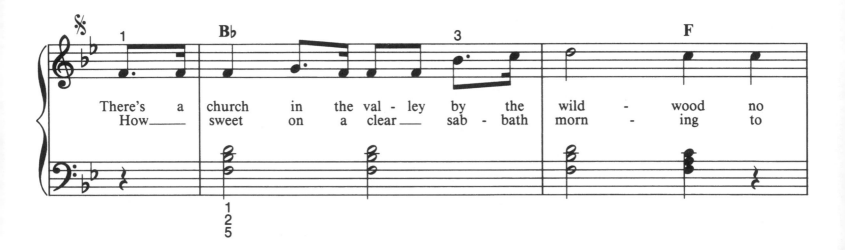

There's a church in the val-ley by the wild - wood no
How___ sweet on a clear___ sab-bath morn - ing to

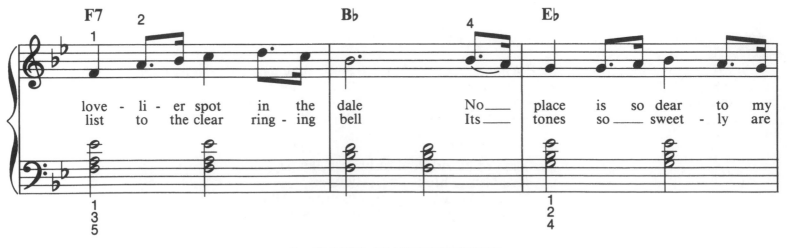

love - li-er spot in the dale
list to the clear ring - ing bell

No___ place is so dear to my
Its___ tones so___ sweet-ly are

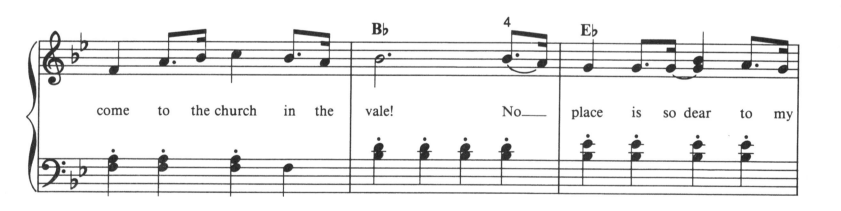

THE CHURCH'S ONE FOUNDATION

Words by SAMUEL JOHN STONE
Music by SAMUEL SEBASTIAN WESLEY

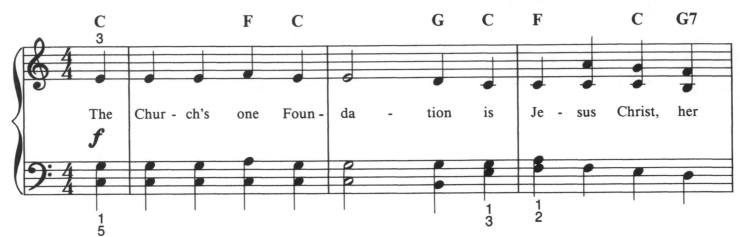

The Chur-ch's one Foun-da - tion is Je-sus Christ, her

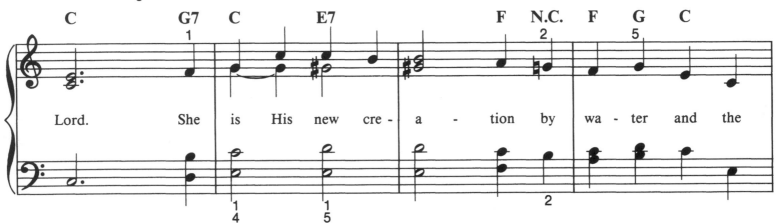

Lord. She is His new cre - a - tion by wa - ter and the

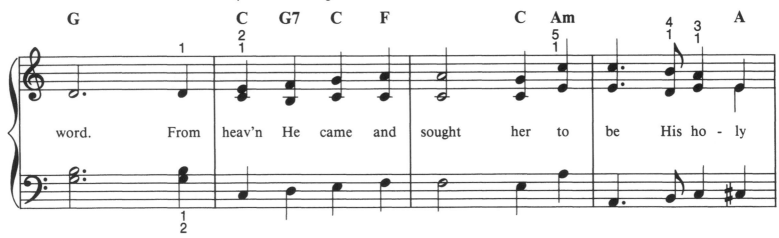

word. From heav'n He came and sought her to be His ho - ly

Bride; With His own blood He bought her, And for her life He died.

COME, CHRISTIANS, JOIN TO SING

Words by CHRISTIAN HENRY BATEMAN
Traditional Spanish Melody

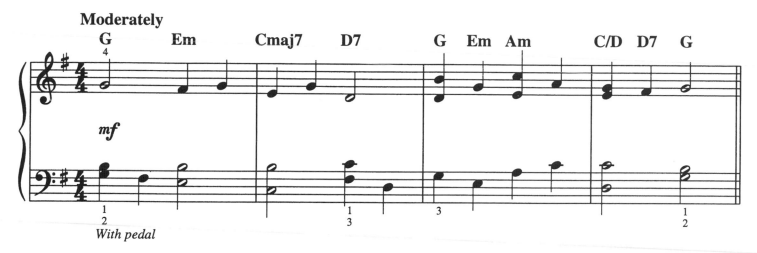

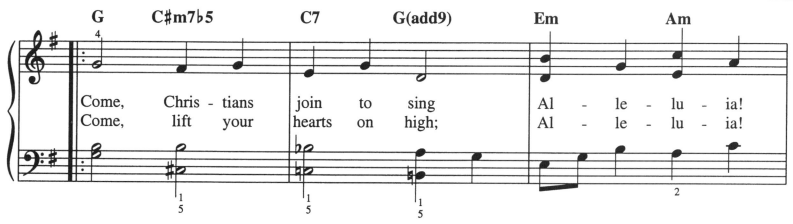

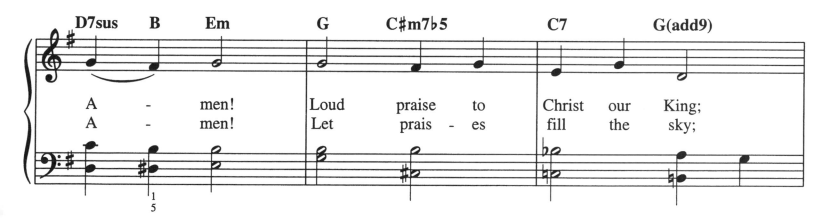

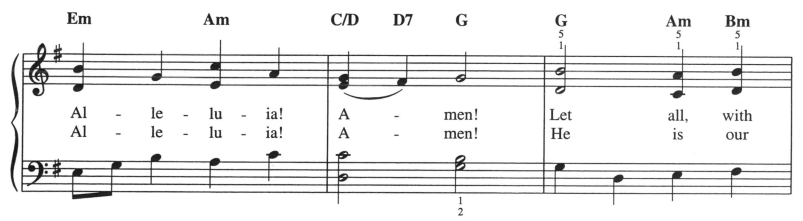

24

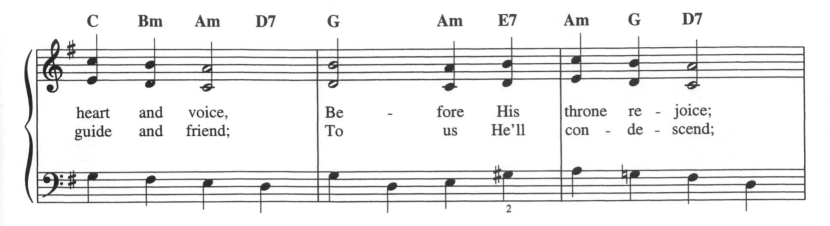

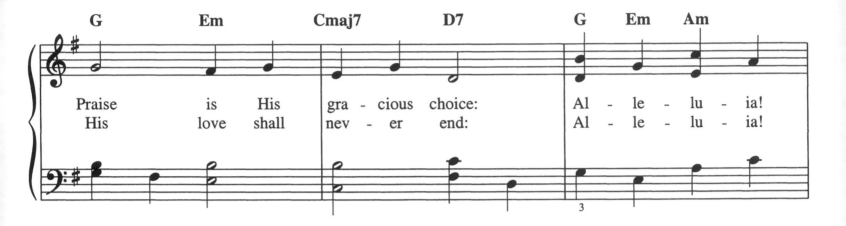

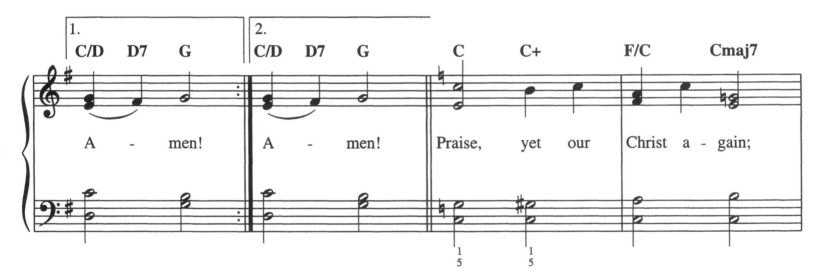

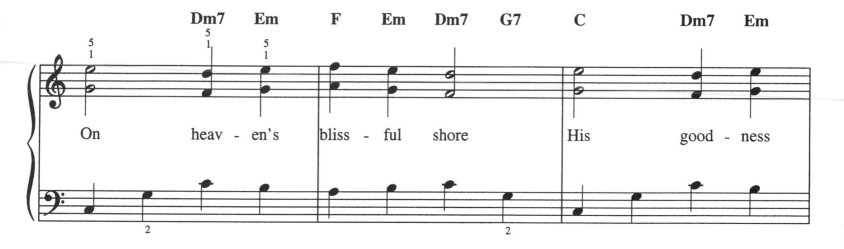

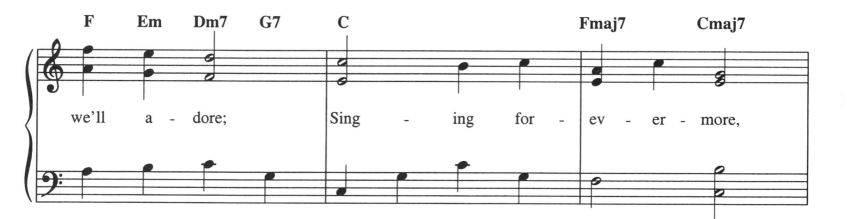

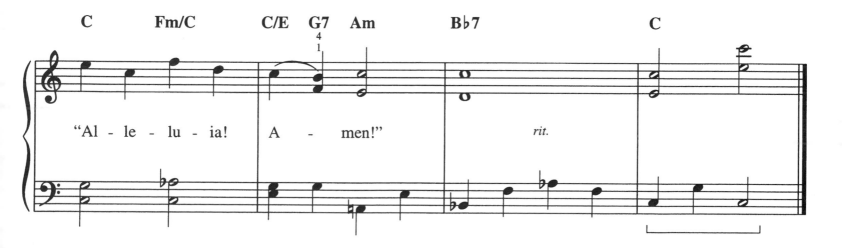

CROWN HIM WITH MANY CROWNS

Words by MATTHEW BRIDGES and GODFREY THRING
Music by GEORGE JOB ELVEY

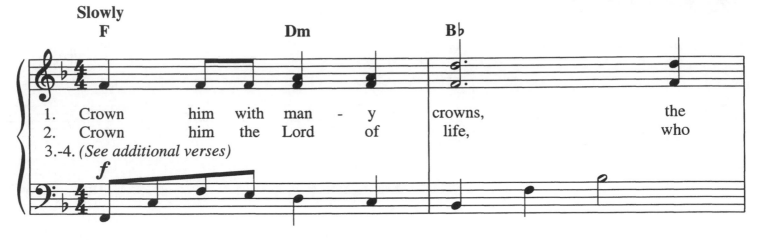

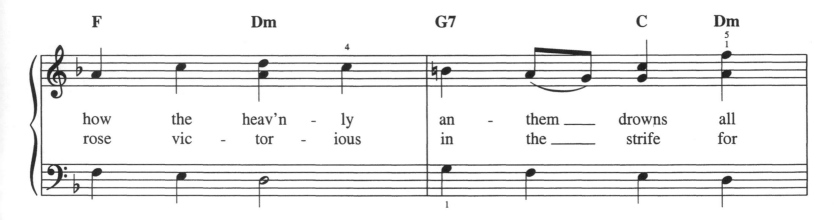

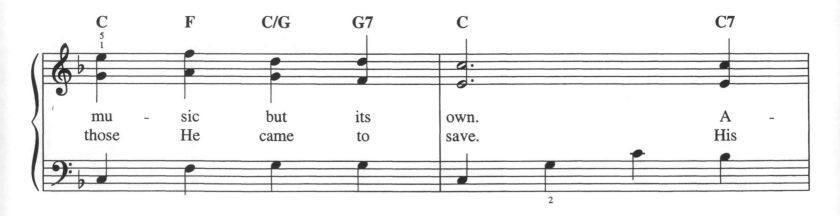

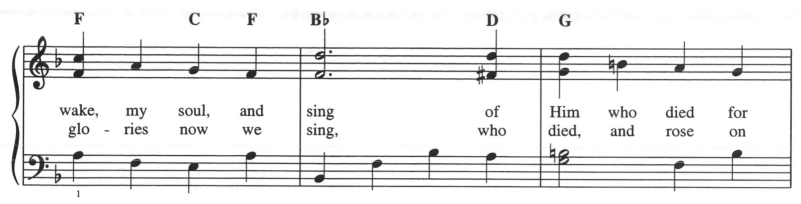

wake, my soul, and sing of Him who died for
glo - ries now we sing, who died, and rose on

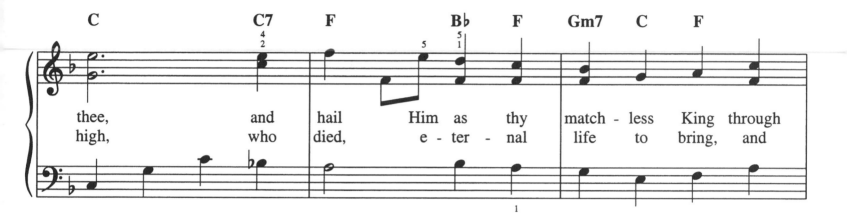

thee, and hail Him as thy match - less King through
high, who died, e - ter - nal life to bring, and

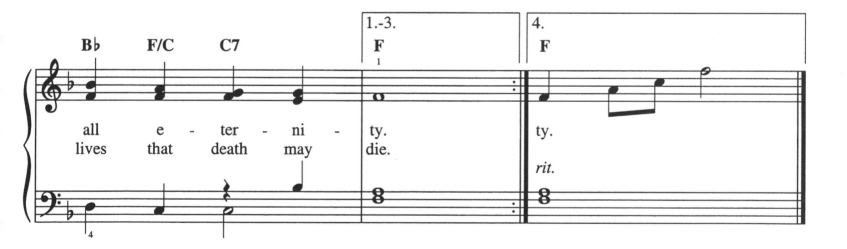

all e - ter - ni - ty. ty.
lives that death may die.

rit.

Additional Verses

3. Crown Him the Lord of peace, whose power a scepter sways
   from pole to pole, that wars may cease, and all be prayer and praise.
   His reign shall know no end, and round His pierced feet
   fair flowers of paradise extend their fragrance ever sweet.

4. Crown Him the Lord of love; behold His hands and side,
   those wounds, yet visible above, in beauty glorified.
   All hail, Redeemer, hail! For Thou hast died for me;
   Thy praise and glory shall not fail throughout eternity.

FAIREST LORD JESUS

Words from *Münster Gesangbuch*
Music from *Schlesische Volkslieder*

Fair - est Lord Je - sus! Ru - ler of all
Fair is the sun - shine, Fair - er still the

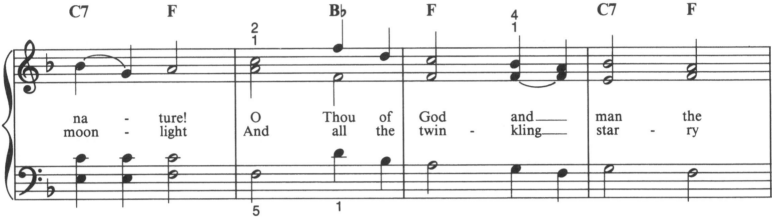

na - ture! O Thou of God and___ man the
moon - light And all the twin - kling___ star - ry

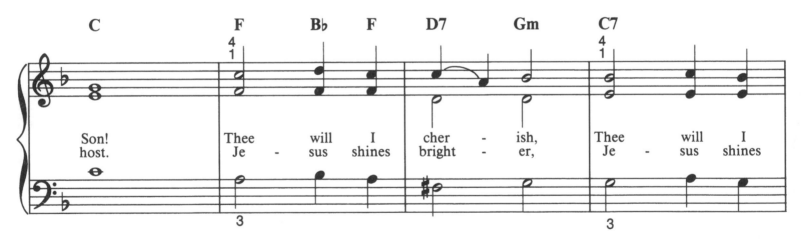

Son! Thee will I cher - ish, Thee will I
host. Je - sus I shines bright - er, Je - sus shines

hon - or, Thou my soul's glo - ry joy and crown.
pur - er Than all the an - gels heav'n and can boast.

HE LEADETH ME

Words by JOSEPH H. GILMORE
Music by WILLIAM B. BRADBURY

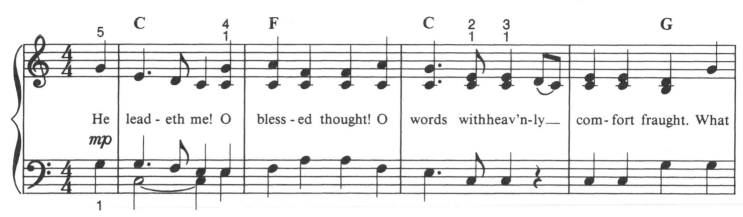

FAITH OF OUR FATHERS

Words by FREDERICK WILLIAM FABER
Music by HENRI F. HEMY

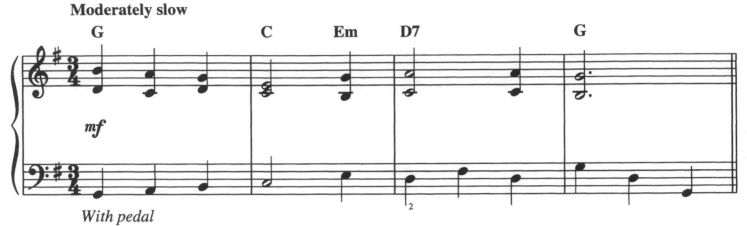

With pedal

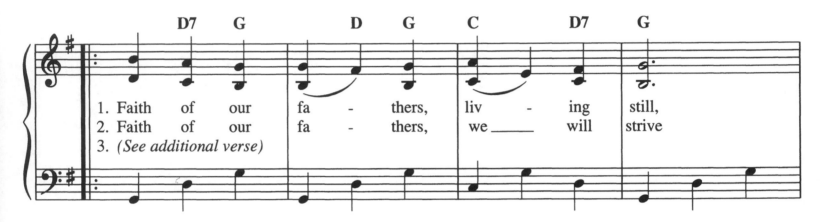

1. Faith of our fa - thers, liv - ing still,
2. Faith of our fa - thers, we ___ will strive
3. (See additional verse)

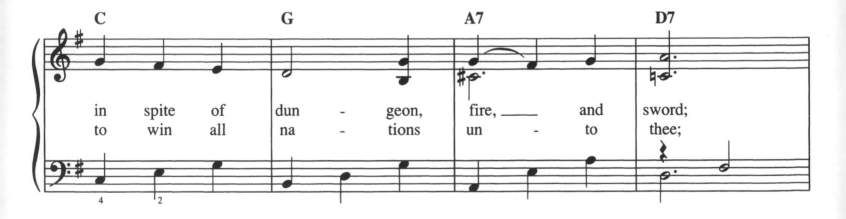

in spite of dun - geon, fire, ___ and sword;
to win all na - tions un - to thee;

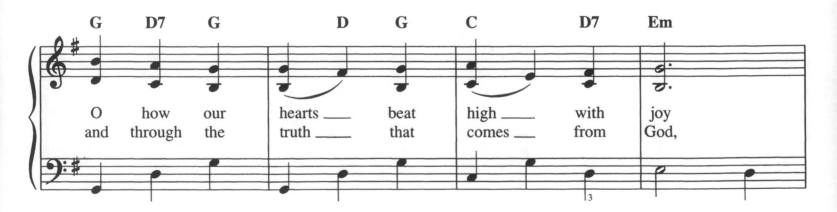

O how our hearts ___ beat high ___ with joy
and through the truth ___ that comes ___ from God,

when e'er we hear that glo - rious word!
we all shall then be tru - ly free.

CHORUS:

Faith of our Fa - thers, ho - ly faith!

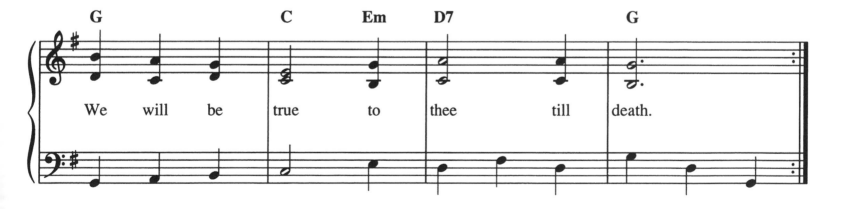

We will be true to thee till death.

Additional Verse

Faith of our fathers, we will love
both friend and foe in all our strife;
and preach thee, too, as love knows how
by kindly words and virtuous life.
To Chorus

FOR ALL THE SAINTS

Words by WILLIAM W. HOW
Music by RALPH VAUGHAN WILLIAMS

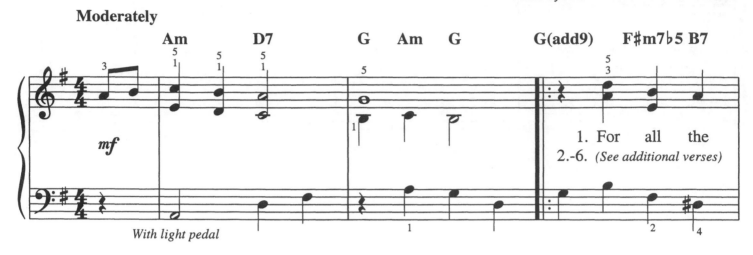

1. For all the
2.-6. *(See additional verses)*

With light pedal

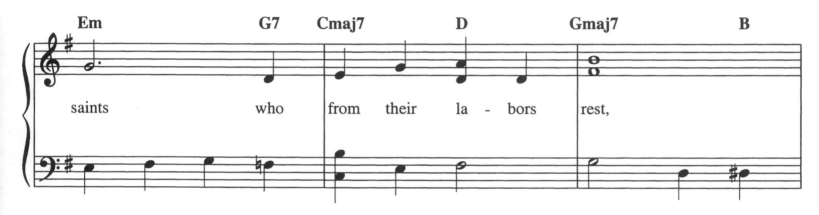

saints who from their la - bors rest,

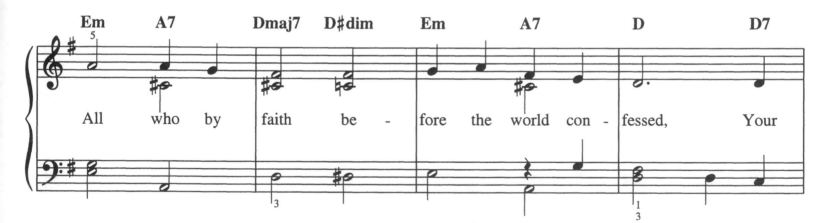

All who by faith be - fore the world con - fessed, Your

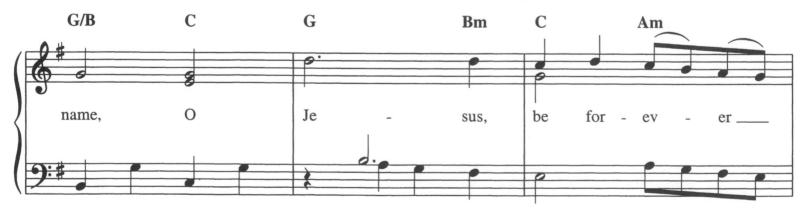

name, O Je - sus, be for - ev - er

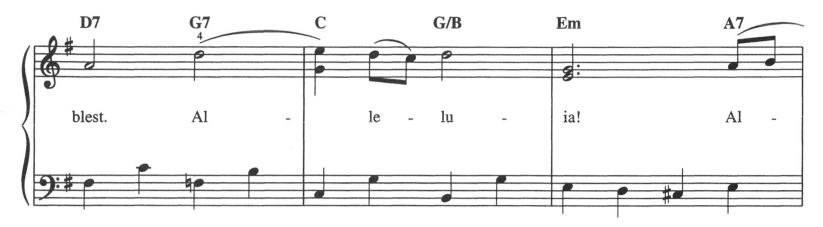

Additional Verses

2. You were their rock, their fortress, and their might;
   You, Lord, their captain in the well-fought fight;
   You, in the darkness drear, their one true light.
   Alleluia! Alleluia!

3. Oh, blest communion, fellowship divine,
   We feebly struggle, they in glory shine;
   Yet all are one within your great design.
   Alleluia! Alleluia!

4. And when the strife is fierce, the warfare long.
   Steals on the ear the distant triumph song,
   And hearts are brave again and arms are strong.
   Alleluia! Alleluia!

5. Oh, may your soldiers, faithful, true and bold,
   Fight as the saints who nobly fought of old
   And win with them the victor's crown of gold.
   Alleluia! Alleluia!

6. The golden evening brightens in the west;
   Soon, soon to faithful warriors comes their rest;
   Sweet is the calm of paradise the blest.
   Alleluia! Alleluia!

FOR THE BEAUTY OF THE EARTH

Words by FOLLIOT S. PIERPOINT
Music by CONRAD KOCHER

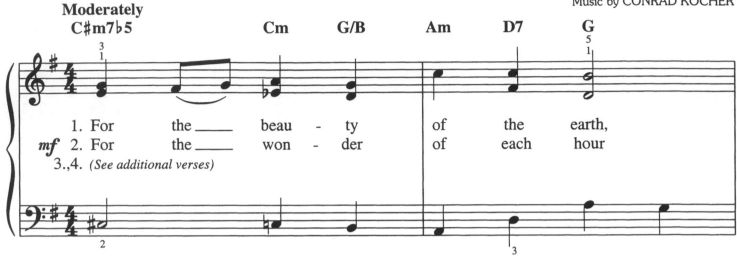

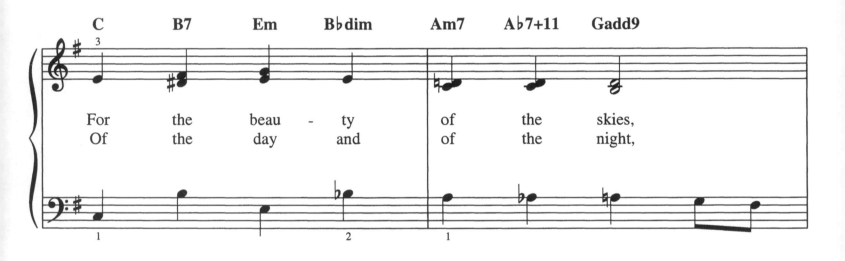

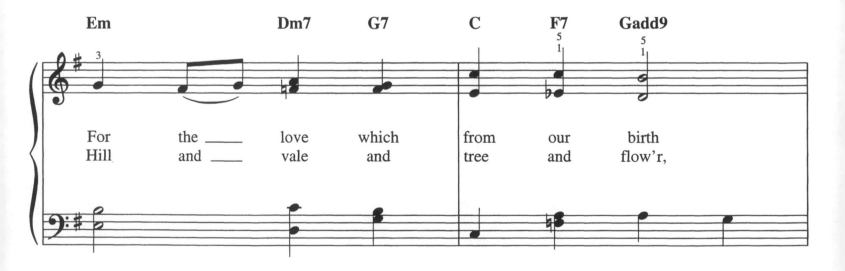

Additional Verses

3. For the joy of ear and eye,
   For the heart and mind's delight,
   For the mystic harmony
   Linking sense to sound and sight:
   Refrain:

4. For the joy of human love,
   Brother, sister, parent, child,
   Friends on earth and friends above;
   For all gentle thoughts and mild;
   Refrain:

GOD OF GRACE AND GOD OF GLORY

Words by HARRY EMERSON FOSDICK
Music by JOHN HUGHES

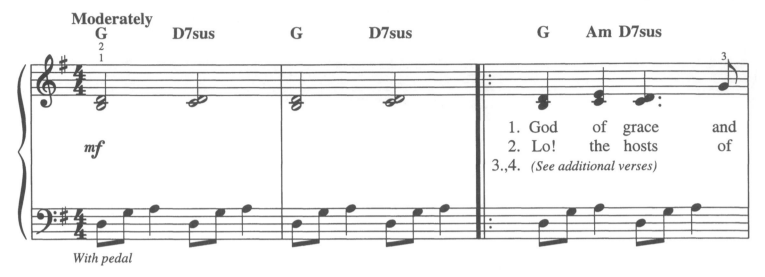

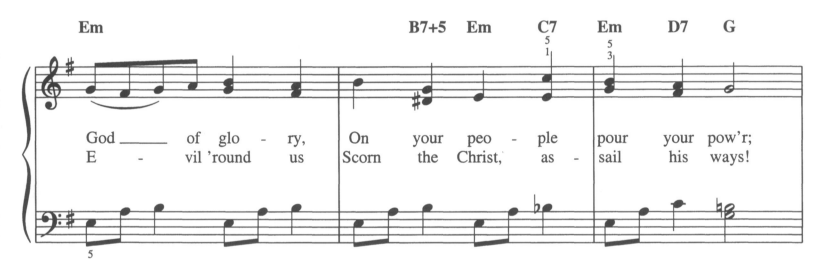

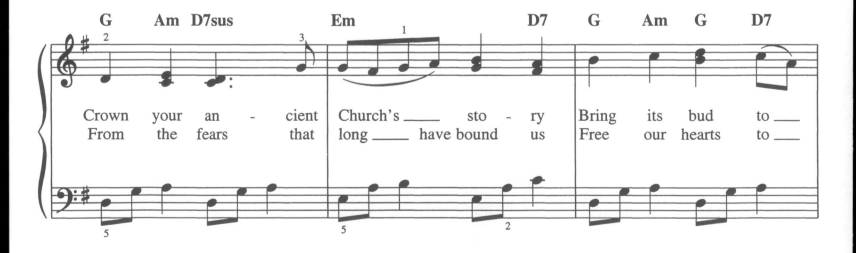

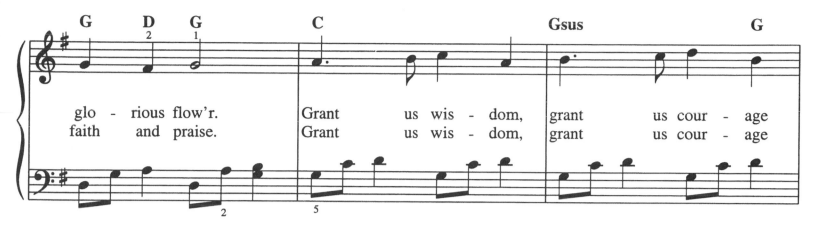

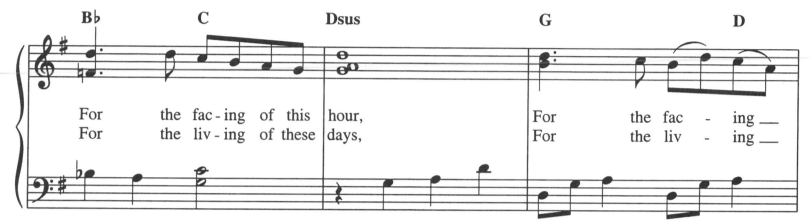

Additional Verses

3. Cure your children's warring madness;
   Bend our pride to your control;
   Shame our wanton, selfish gladness,
   Rich in things and poor in soul.
   Grant us wisdom, grant us courage,
   Lest we miss your kingdom's goal,
   Lest we miss your kingdom's goal.

4. Save us from weak resignation
   To the evils we deplore;
   Let the gift of your salvation
   Be our glory evermore.
   Grant us wisdom, grant us courage,
   Serving you whom we adore,
   Serving you whom we adore.

GOD OF OUR FATHERS

Words by DANIEL CRANE ROBERTS
Music by GEORGE WILLIAM WARREN

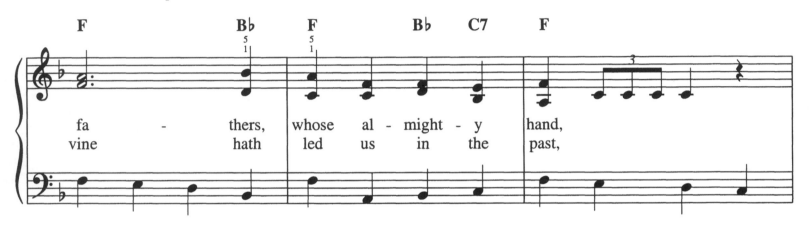

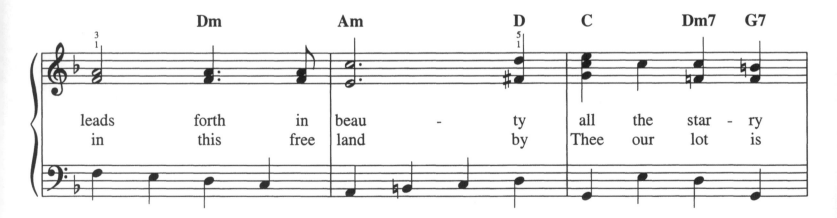

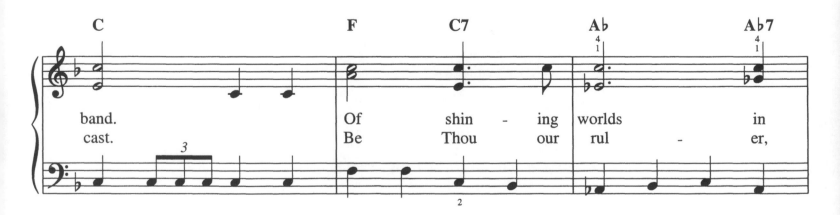

GOD OF OUR FATHERS

Words by DANIEL CRANE ROBERTS
Music by GEORGE WILLIAM WARREN

Majestically

With pedal

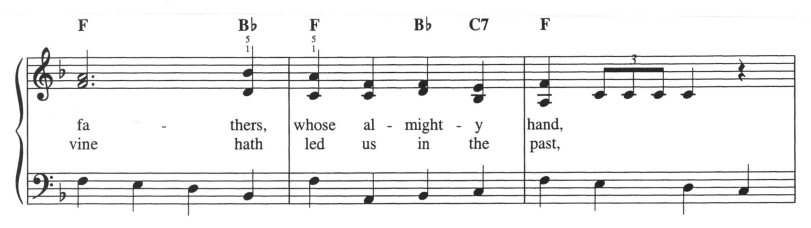

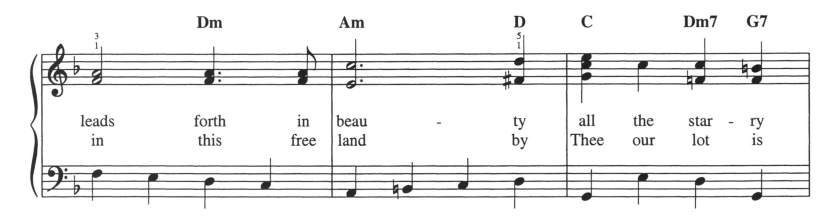

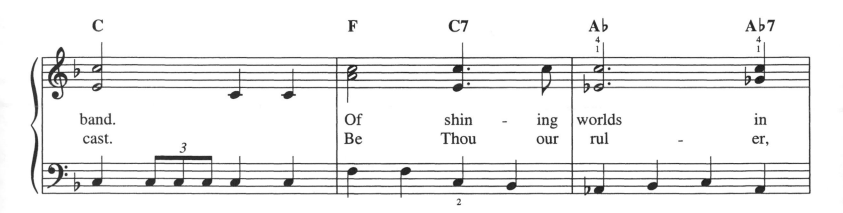

glo - rious flow'r.
faith and praise.
Grant us wis - dom, grant us cour - age
Grant us wis - dom, grant us cour - age

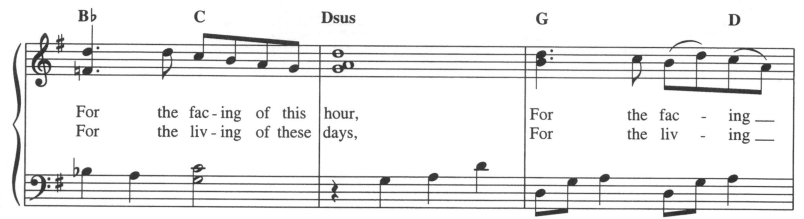

For the fac-ing of this hour,
For the liv-ing of these days,
For the fac - ing ___
For the liv - ing ___

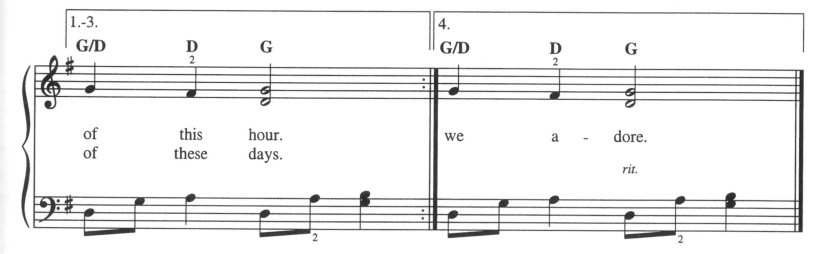

1.-3.
of this hour.
of these days.

4.
we a - dore.
rit.

Additional Verses

3. Cure your children's warring madness;
   Bend our pride to your control;
   Shame our wanton, selfish gladness,
   Rich in things and poor in soul.
   Grant us wisdom, grant us courage,
   Lest we miss your kingdom's goal,
   Lest we miss your kingdom's goal.

4. Save us from weak resignation
   To the evils we deplore;
   Let the gift of your salvation
   Be our glory evermore.
   Grant us wisdom, grant us courage,
   Serving you whom we adore,
   Serving you whom we adore.

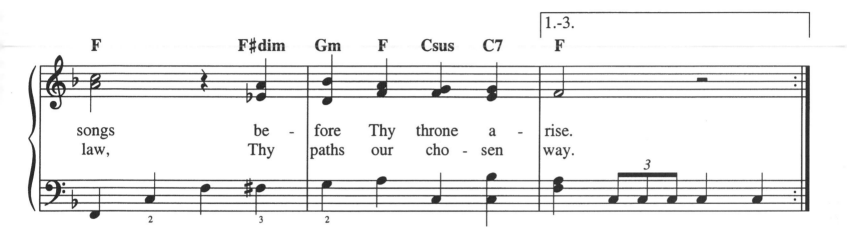

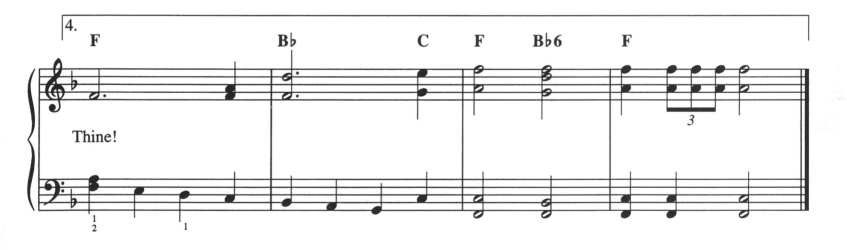

Additional Verses

3. From war's alarms, from deadly pestilence,
Be Thy strong arm our ever sure defense.
Thy true religion in our hearts increase,
Thy bounteous goodness nourish us in peace.

4. Refresh Thy people on their toilsome way,
Lead us from night to never ending day.
Fill all our lives with love and grace divine,
And glory, laud, and praise be ever Thine! Amen.

HEAVENLY SUNLIGHT

Words by HENRY J. ZELLEY
Music by GEORGE HARRISON COOK

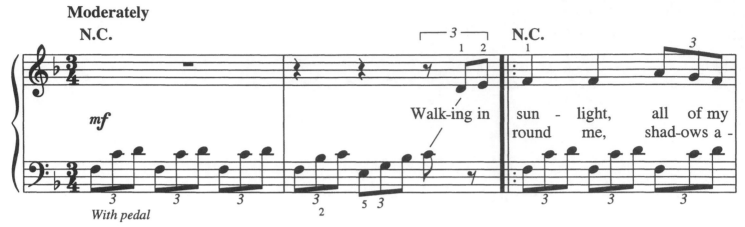

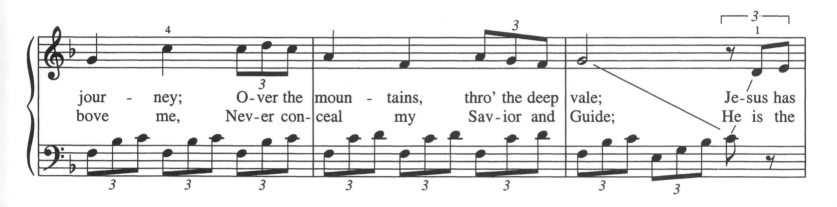

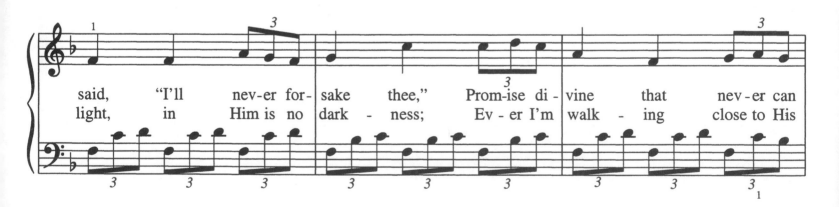

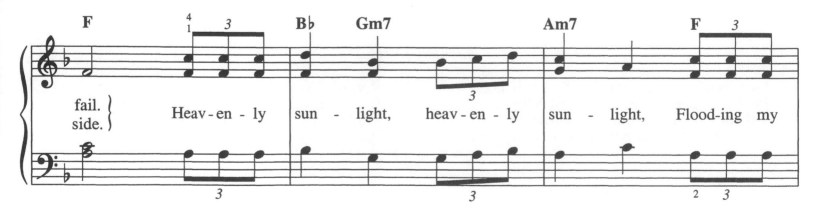

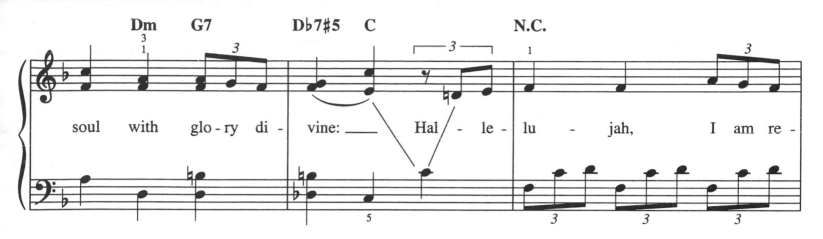

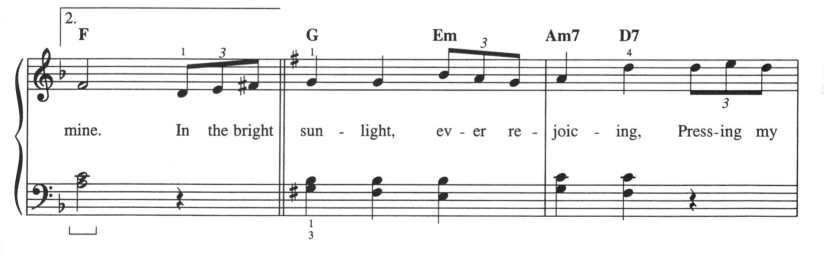

42

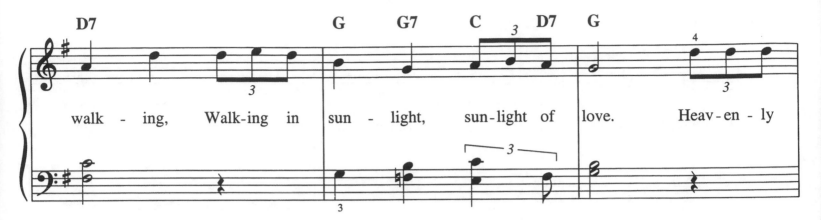

walk - ing, Walk-ing in sun - light, sun-light of love. Heav-en - ly

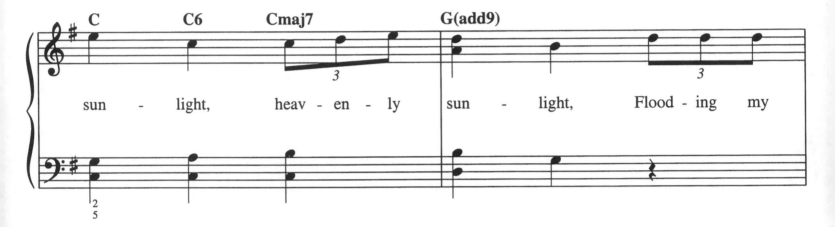

sun - light, heav-en - ly sun - light, Flood - ing my

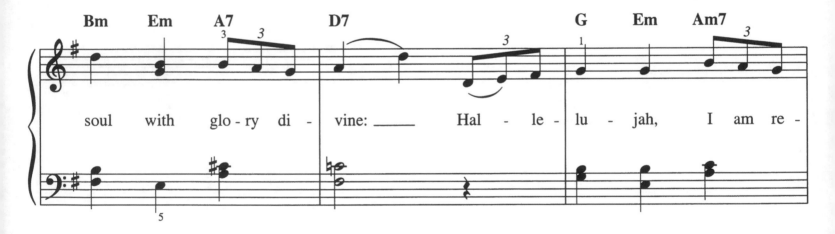

soul with glo-ry di - vine: _____ Hal - le - lu - jah, I am re -

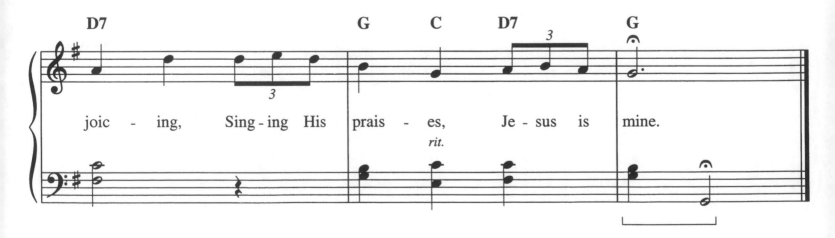

joic - ing, Sing-ing His prais - es, Je - sus is mine.

rit.

HOLY GOD, WE PRAISE THY NAME

Words and Music from *Katholisches Gesangbuch*
Words attributed to IGNAZ FRANZ
Translated by CLARENCE WALWORTH

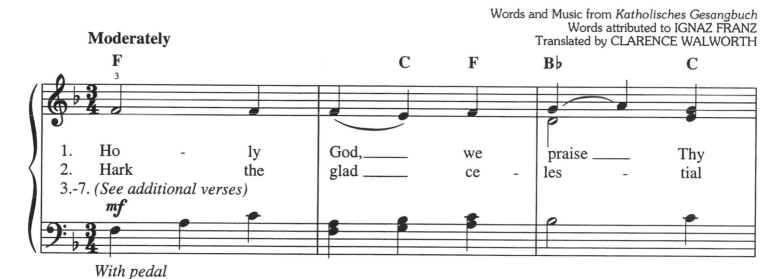

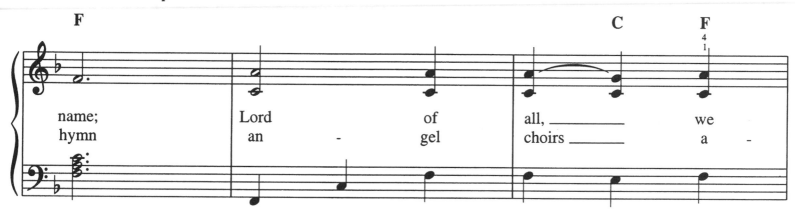

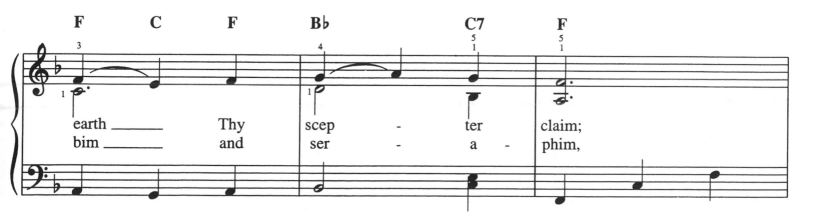

44

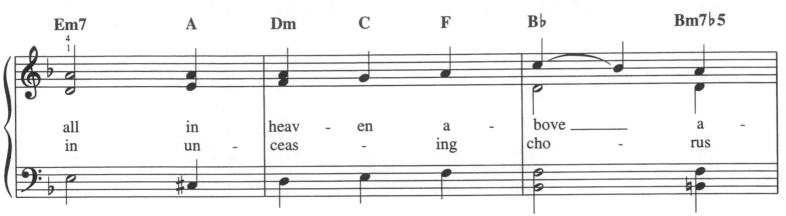

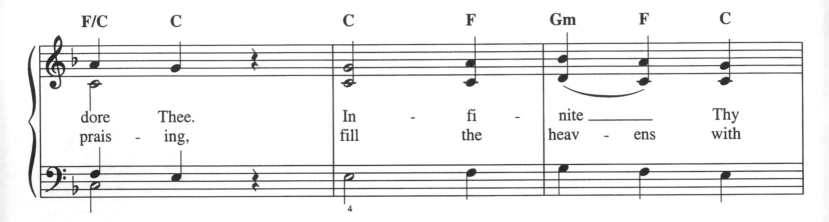

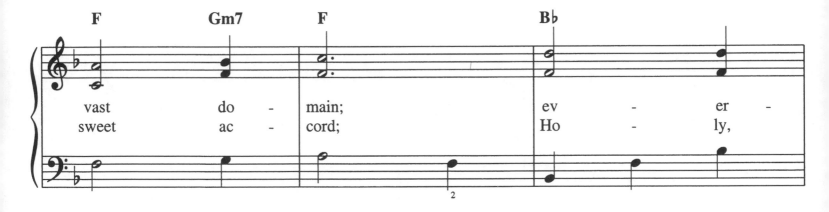

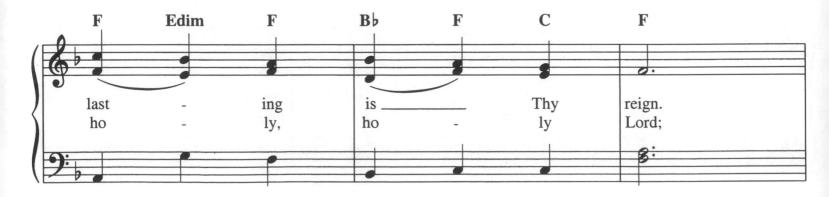

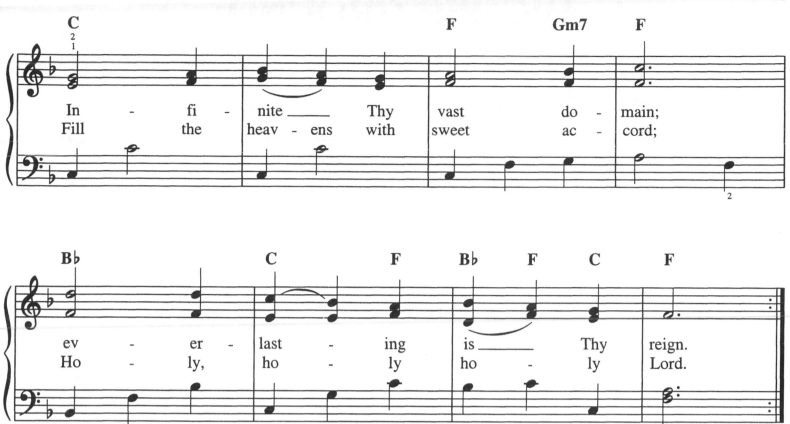

In - fi - nite _____ Thy vast do - main;
Fill the heav - ens with sweet ac - cord;

ev - er - last - ing is _____ Thy reign.
Ho - ly, ho - ly ho - ly Lord.

Additional Verses

3. Lo! the apostolic train
   joins thy sacred name to hallow;
   prophets swell the glad refrain,
   and the white-robed martyrs follow.
   And from morn to set of sun,
   through the church the song goes on.
   And from morn to set of sun,
   through the church the song goes on.

4. Holy Father, Holy Son,
   Holy Spirit: three we name Thee,
   though in essence only one;
   undivided God we claim Thee,
   and adoring bend the knee
   while we own the mystery;
   and adoring bend the knee
   while we own the mystery.

5. Christ, Thou art our glorious King,
   Son of God, enthroned in splendor;
   but deliverance to bring
   Thou all honors didst surrender,
   and wast of a virgin born
   humbly on that blessed morn;
   and wast of a virgin born
   humbly on that blessed morn.

6. Thou didst take the sting from death,
   Son of God, as Savior given;
   on the cross Thy dying breath
   opened wide the realm of heaven.
   In the glory of that land
   Thou art set at God's right hand.
   In the glory of that land
   Thou art set at God's right hand.

7. As our judge Thou wilt appear,
   Savior, who hast died to win us;
   help Thy servants, drawing near;
   Lord, renew our hearts within us.
   Grant that with Thy saints we may
   dwell in everlasting day.
   Grant that with Thy saints we may
   dwell in everlasting day.

HIGHER GROUND

Words by JOHNSON OATMAN, JR.
Music by CHARLES H. GABRIEL

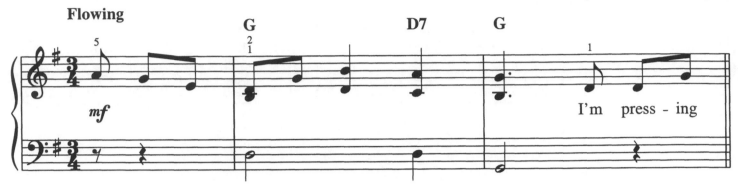

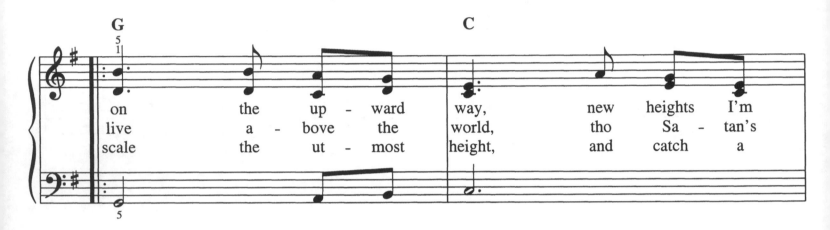

I'm press - ing

on   the   up - ward   way,   new   heights   I'm
live   a - bove   the   world,   tho   Sa -   tan's
scale   the   ut - most   height,   and   catch   a

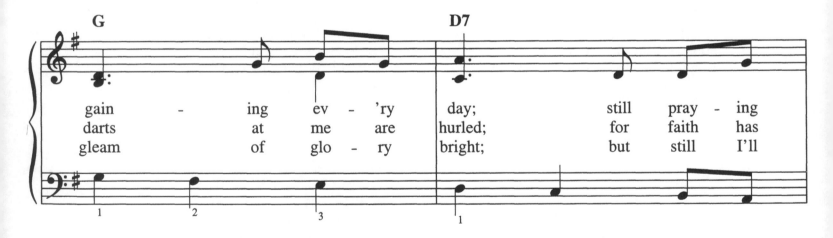

gain - ing   ev - 'ry   day;   still   pray - ing
darts   at   me   are   hurled;   for   faith   has
gleam   of   glo - ry   bright;   but   still   I'll

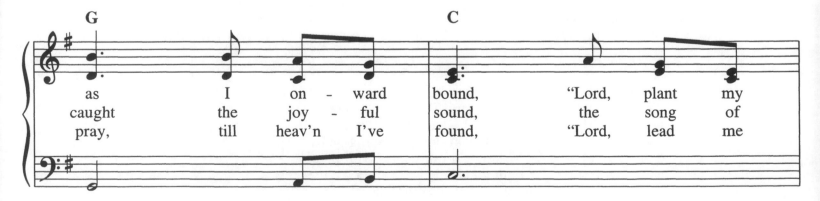

as   I   on - ward   bound,   "Lord,   plant   my
caught   the   joy - ful   sound,   the   song   of
pray,   till   heav'n   I've   found,   "Lord,   lead   me

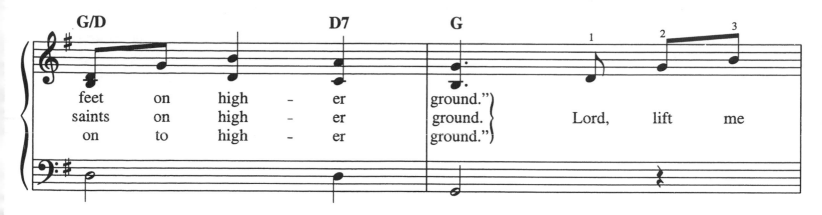

feet on high - er ground."}
saints on high - er ground. }
on to high - er ground."}
Lord, lift me

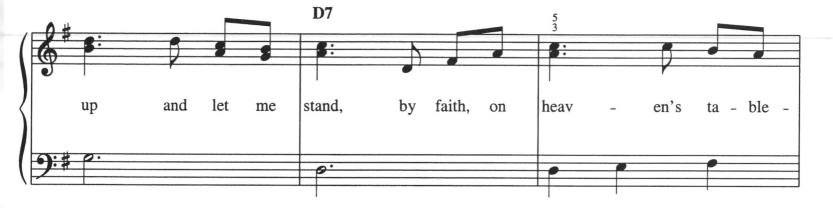

up and let me stand, by faith, on heav - en's ta - ble -

land; a high - er plane than I have found. Lord, plant my

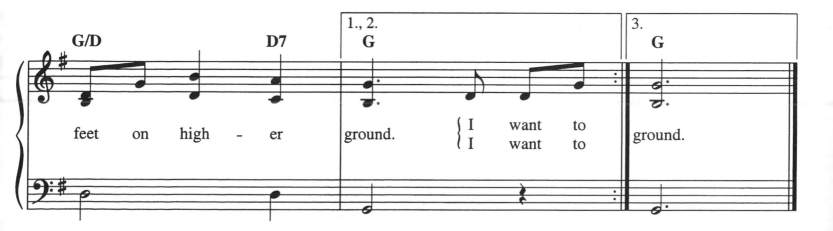

feet on high - er ground.
1., 2.
{ I want to
{ I want to
3.
ground.

HOLY, HOLY, HOLY

Text by REGINALD HEBER
Music by JOHN B. DYKES

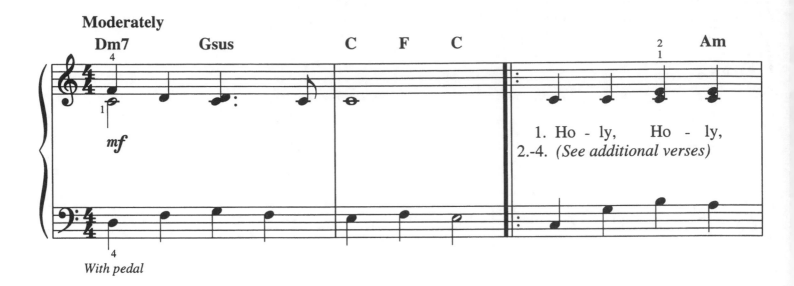

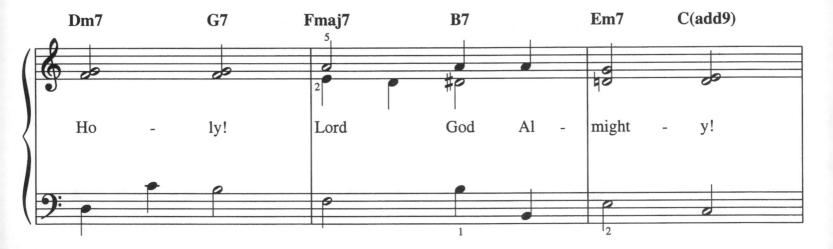

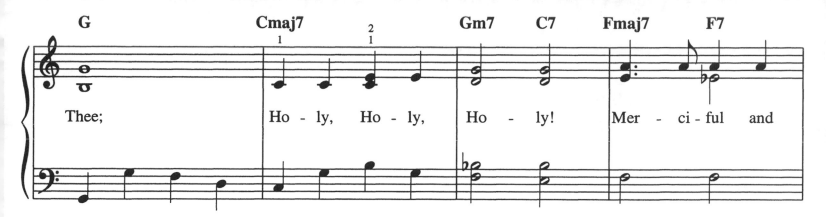

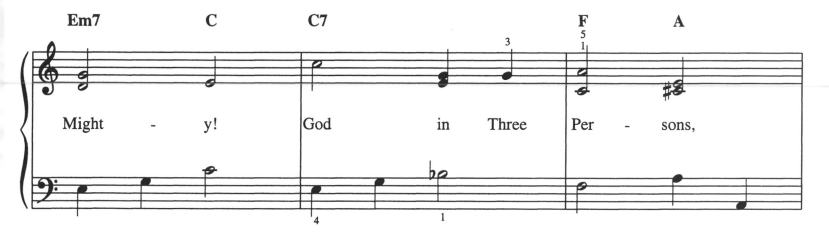

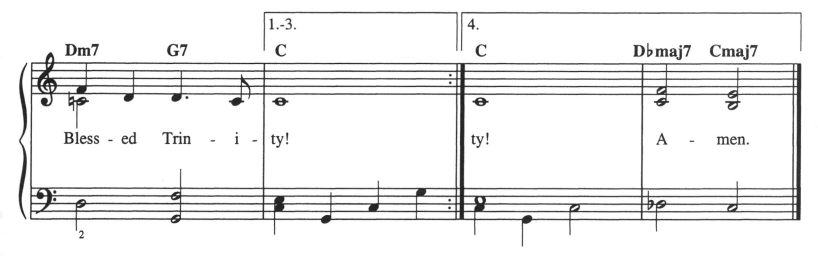

Additional Verses

2. Holy, Holy, Holy! All the saints adore Thee,
   Casting down their golden crowns around the glassy sea;
   Cherubim and seraphim falling down before Thee,
   Who wert, and art, and evermore shalt be.

3. Holy, Holy, Holy! Though the darkness hide Thee,
   Though the eye of sinful man Thy glory may not see,
   Only Thou art holy; there is none beside Thee
   Perfect in power, in love, and purity.

4. Holy, Holy, Holy! Lord God Almighty!
   All Thy works shall praise Thy Name, in earth and sky and sea;
   Holy, Holy, Holy! Merciful and Mighty!
   God in Three Persons, blessed Trinity! Amen.

I LOVE TO TELL THE STORY

Words by A. CATHERINE HANKEY
Music by WILLIAM G. FISCHER

Moderately slow

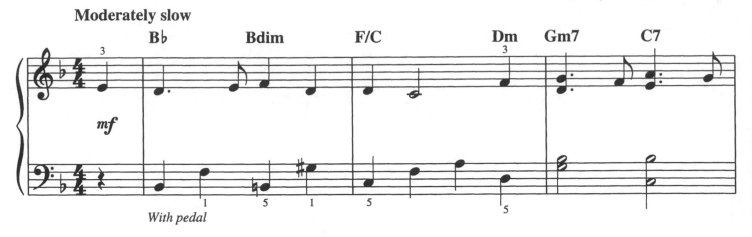

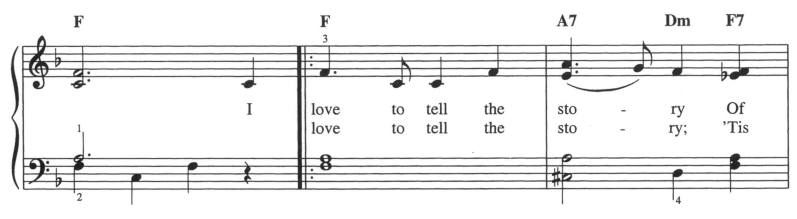

I love to tell the sto - ry Of
love to tell the sto - ry; 'Tis

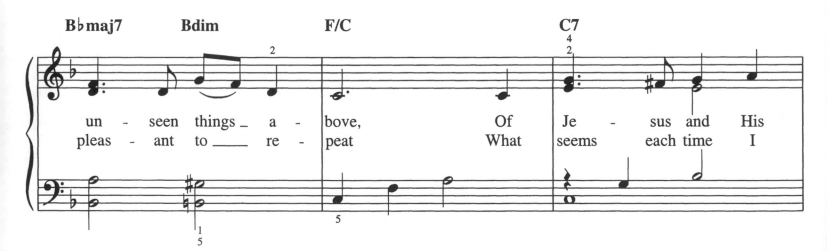

un - seen things __ a - bove, Of Je - sus and His
pleas - ant to __ re - peat What seems each time I

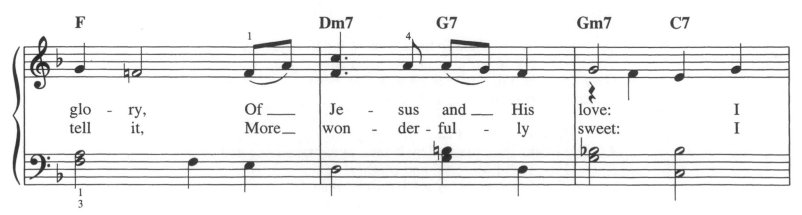

glo - ry, Of __ Je - sus and __ His love: I
tell it, More __ won - der - ful - ly sweet: I

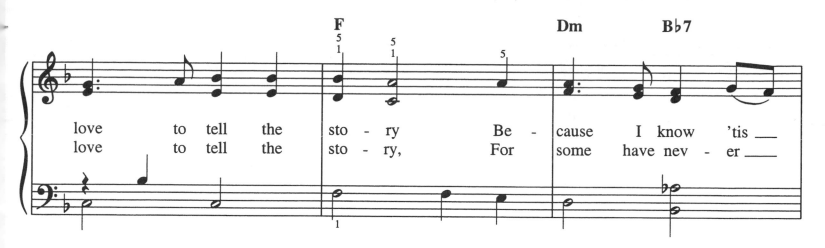

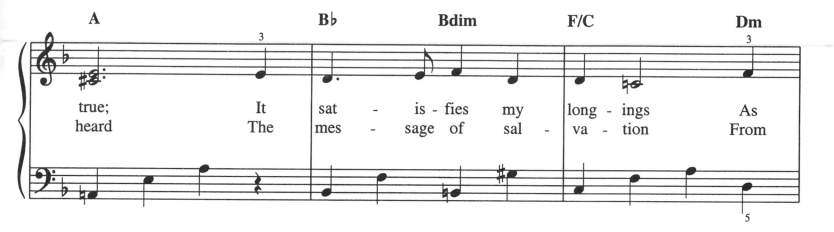

52

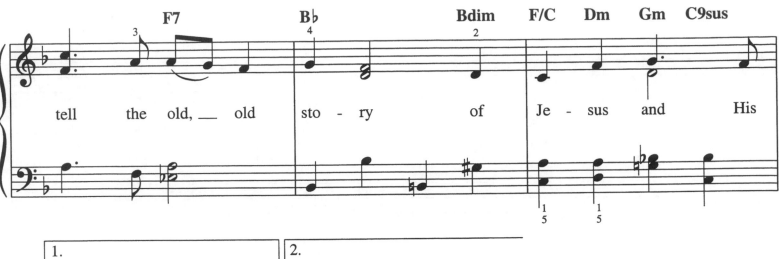

tell the old, — old sto - ry of Je - sus and His

1.
love. I
2.
love. I love to tell the

sto - ry; For those who know — it best Seem

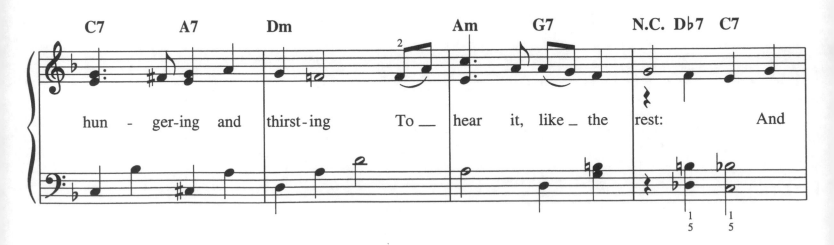

hun - ger-ing and thirst-ing To — hear it, like — the rest: And

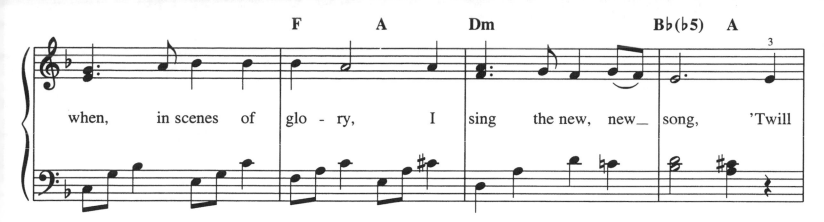

when, in scenes of glo - ry, I sing the new, new_ song, 'Twill

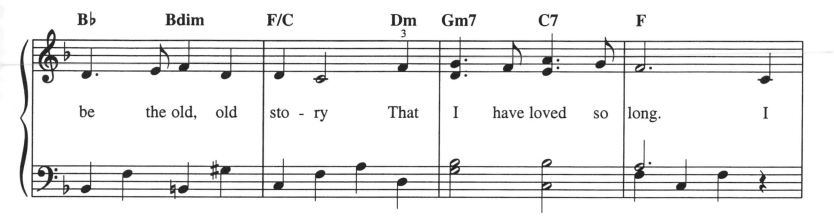

be the old, old sto - ry That I have loved so long. I

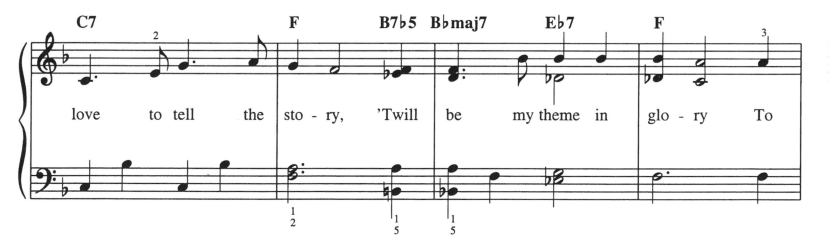

love to tell the sto - ry, 'Twill be my theme in glo - ry To

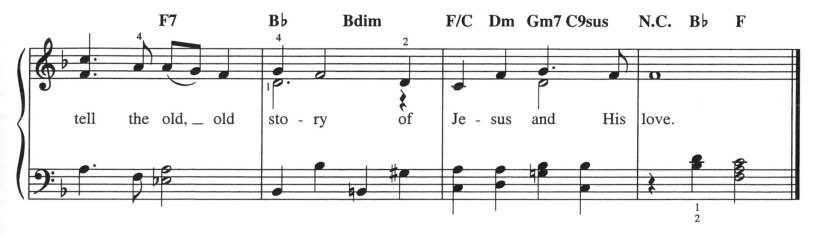

tell the old, _ old sto - ry of Je - sus and His love.

I NEED THEE EVERY HOUR

Words by ANNIE S. HAWKS
Music by ROBERT LOWRY

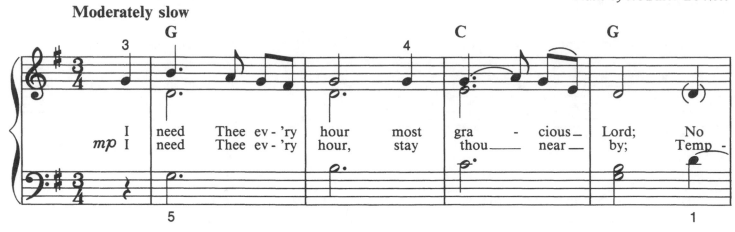

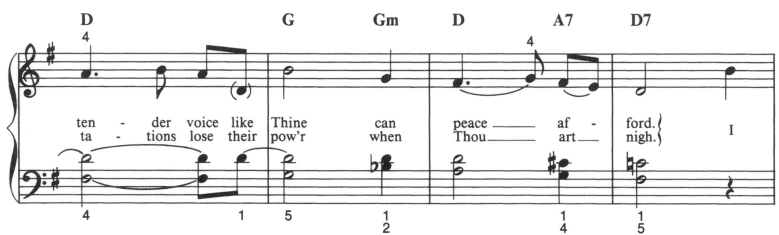

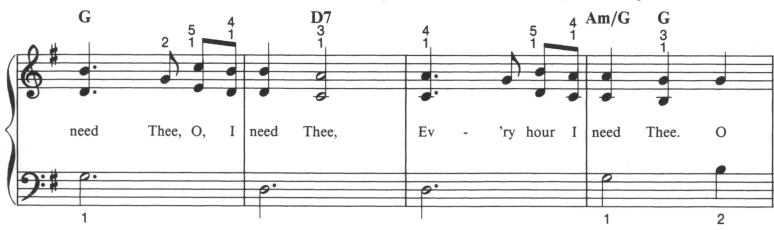

LEAD ON, O KING ETERNAL

Words by ERNEST W. SHURTLEFF
Music by HENRY T. SMART

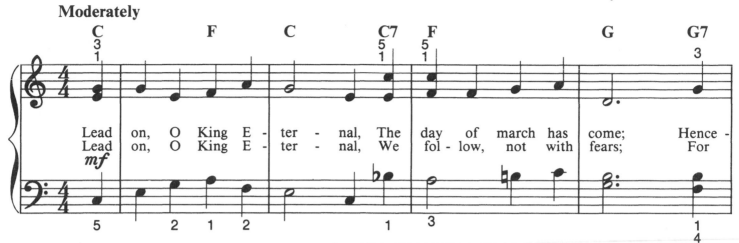

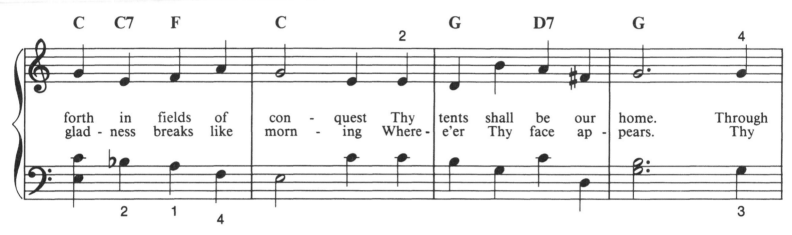

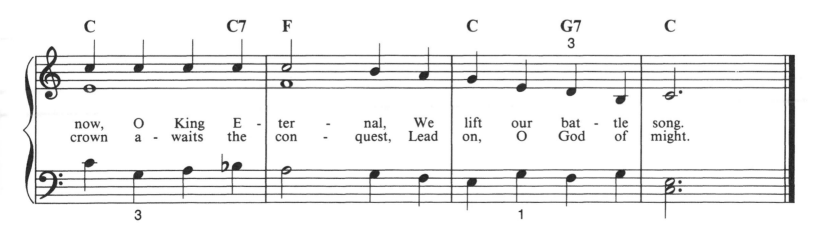

JESUS LOVES ME

Words by ANNA B. WARNER
Music by WILLIAM B. BRADBURY

With expression

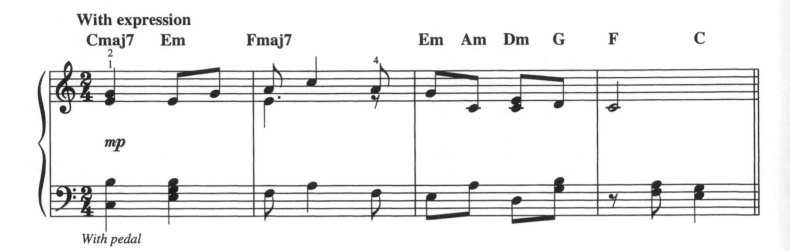

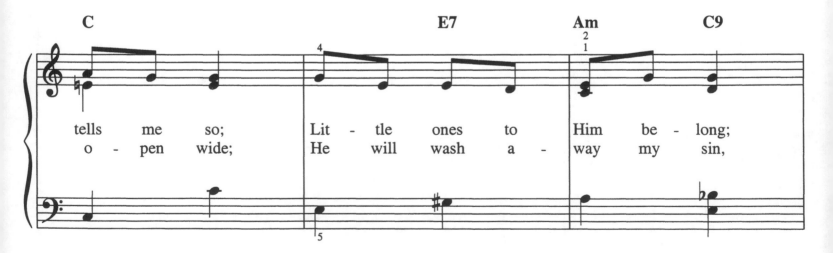

57

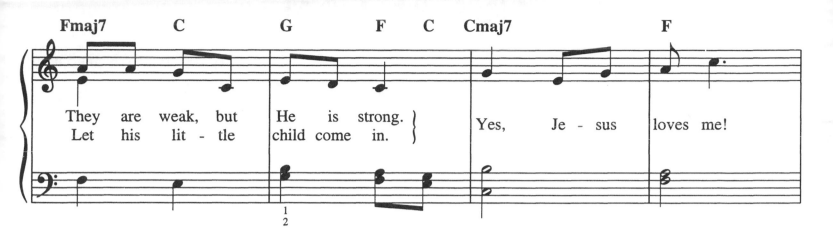

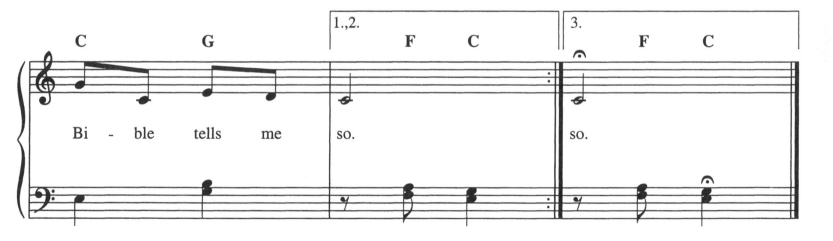

Additional Verse

3. Jesus, take this heart of mine,
   Make it pure and wholly Thine,
   Thou hast bled and died for me;
   I will henceforth live for Thee.
   Yes, Jesus loves me!
   Yes, Jesus loves me!
   Yes, Jesus loves me!
   The Bible tells me so.

JUST AS I AM

Words by CHARLOTTE ELLIOTT
Music by WILLIAM B. BRADBURY

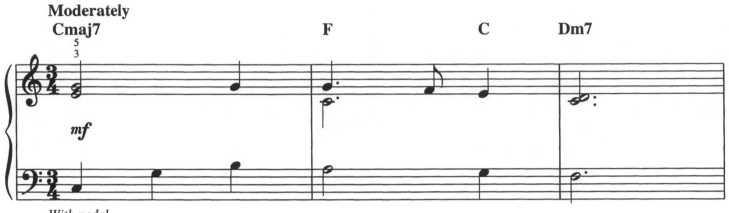

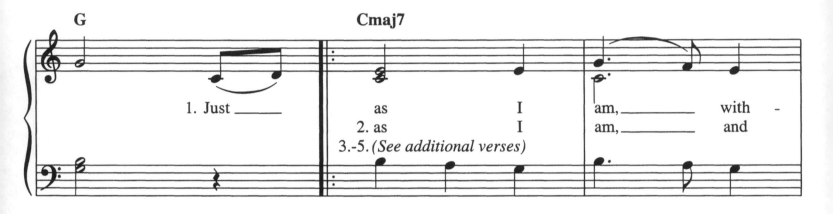

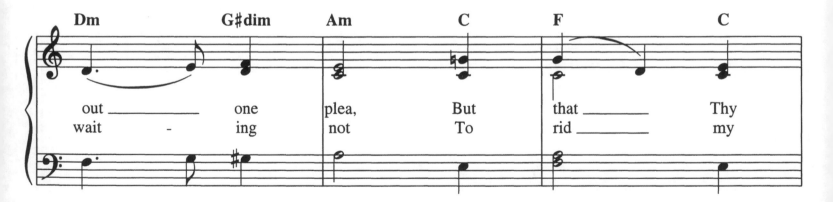

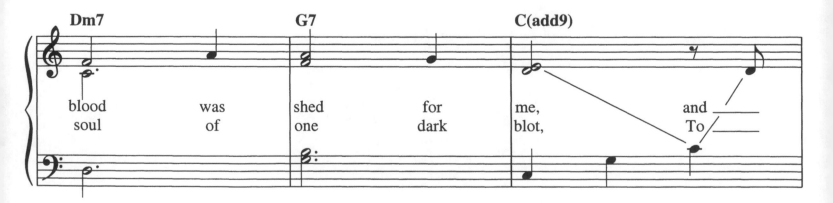

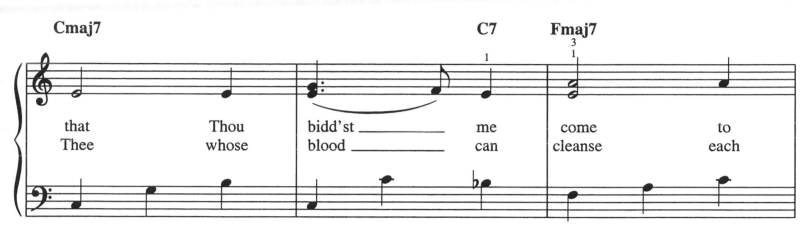

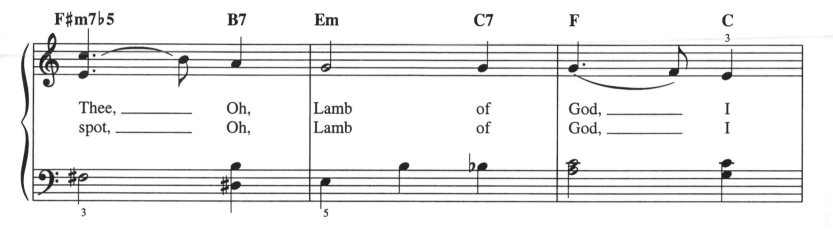

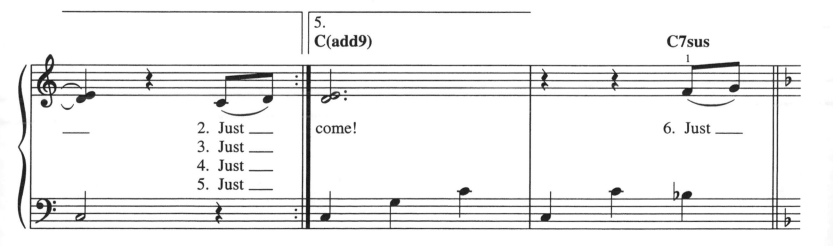

as I am, _____ Thy love _____ un -

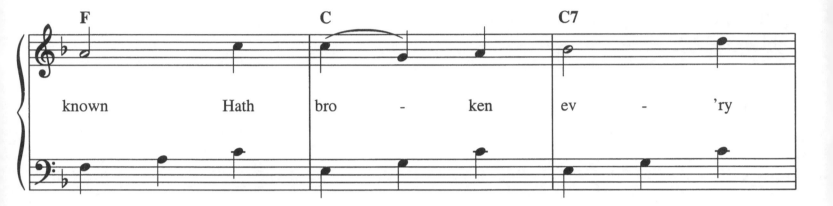

known Hath bro - ken ev - 'ry

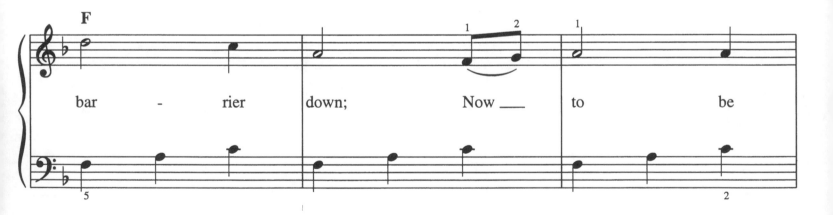

bar - rier down; Now ___ to be

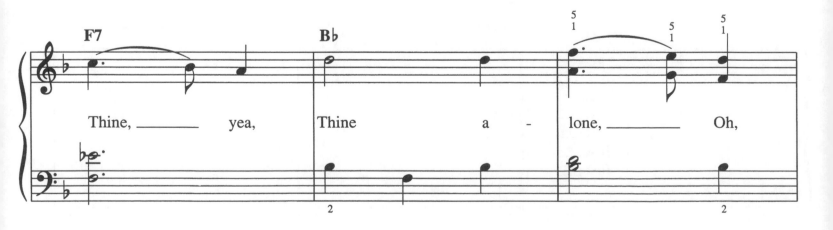

Thine, _____ yea, Thine a - lone, _____ Oh,

Am7   **Dm7**   **Gm7/C**

Lamb   of   God, _____ I   come!

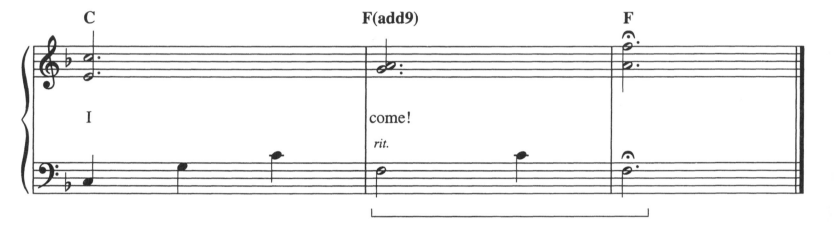

C   **F(add9)**   **F**

I   come!

rit.

Additional Verses

3. Just as I am, tho' tossed about
   With many a conflict, many a doubt,
   Fightings within and fears without,
   Oh, Lamb of God, I come! I come!

4. Just as I am, poor, wretched, blind;
   Sight, riches, healing of the mind,
   Yea, all I need in Thee to find,
   Oh, Lamb of God, I come! I come!

5. Just as I am, Thou wilt receive,
   Wilt welcome, pardon, cleanse, relieve,
   Because Thy promise I believe,
   Oh, Lamb of God, I come! I come!

LEANING ON THE EVERLASTING ARMS

Words by ELISHA A. HOFFMAN
Music by ANTHONY J. SHOWALTER

Chorus

Lean - ing, lean - ing, safe and se - cure from

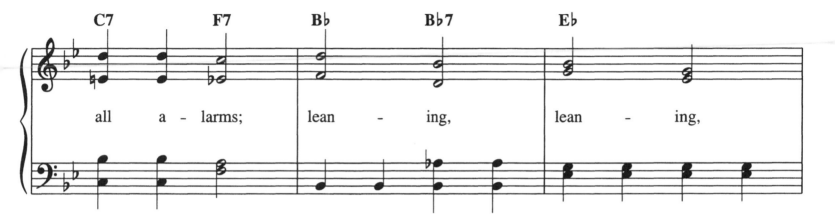

all a - larms; lean - ing, lean - ing,

lean - ing on the ev - er - last - ing arms. last - ing arms.

Additional Verse

3. What have I to dread, what have I to fear,
   Leaning on the everlasting arms?
   I have blessed peace with my Lord so near,
   Leaning on the everlasting arms.
   Chorus

LET US BREAK BREAD TOGETHER

Traditional Spiritual

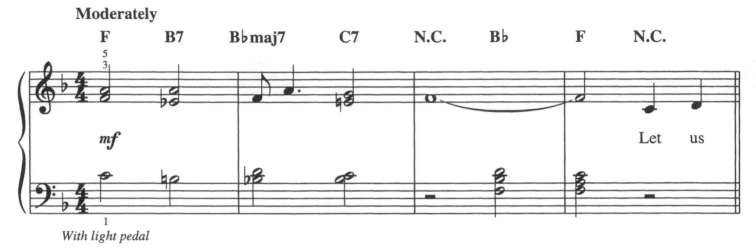

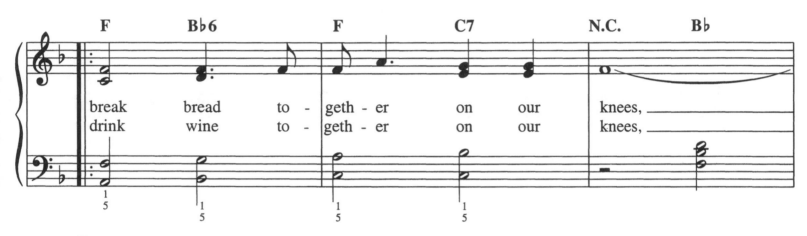

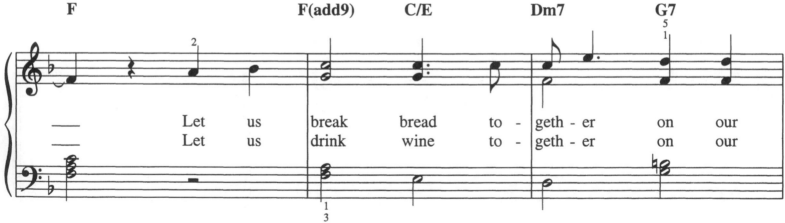

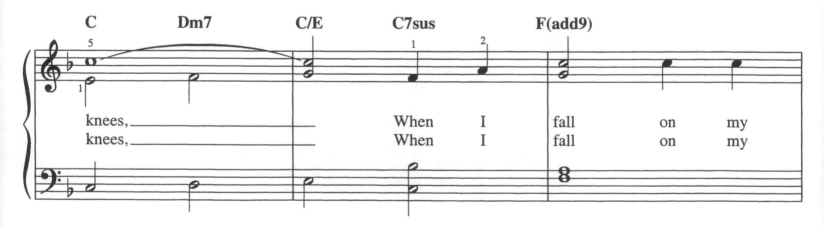

knees with my face to the ris - ing sun, Oh
knees with my face to the ris - ing sun, Oh

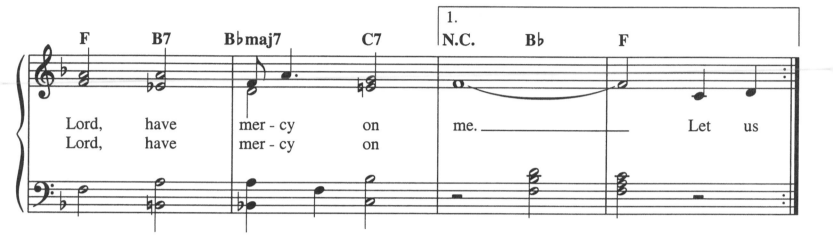

1.

Lord, have mer - cy on me. _____ Let us
Lord, have mer - cy on

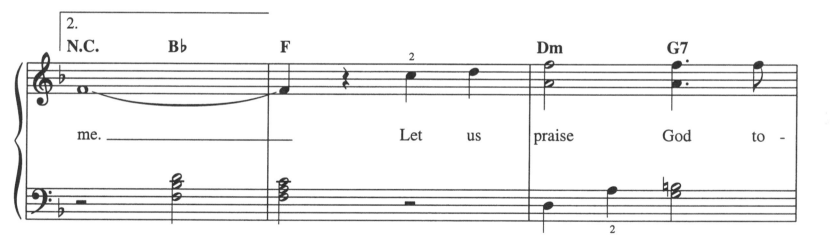

2.

me. _____ Let us praise God to -

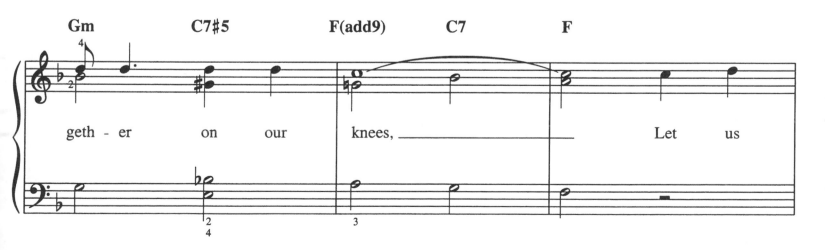

geth - er on our knees, _____ Let us

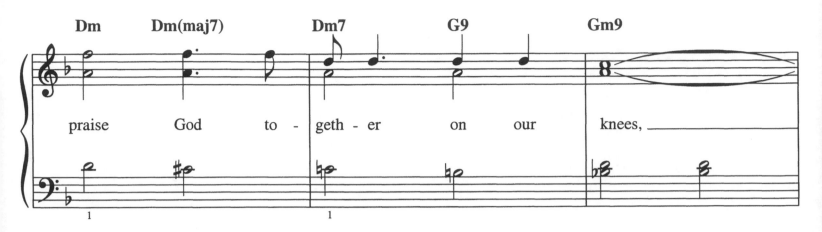

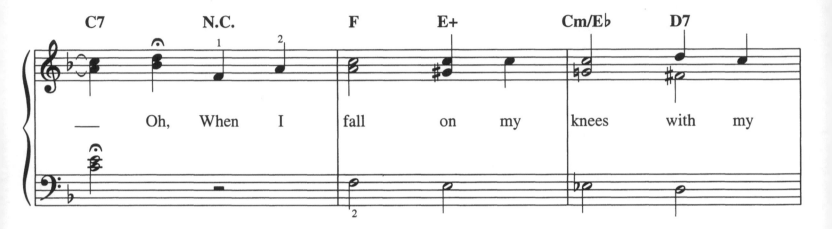

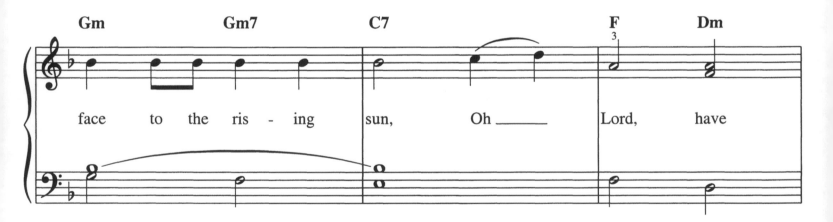

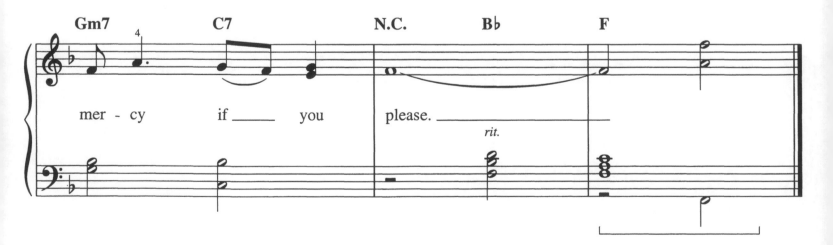

NOW THANK WE ALL OUR GOD

German Words by MARTIN RINKART
English Translation by CATHERINE WINKWORTH
Music by JOHANN CRÜGER

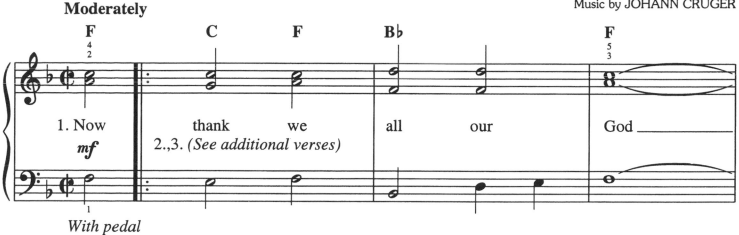

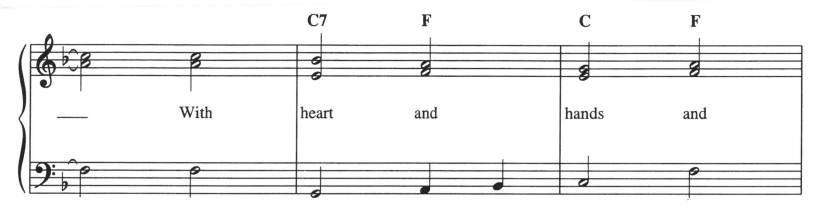

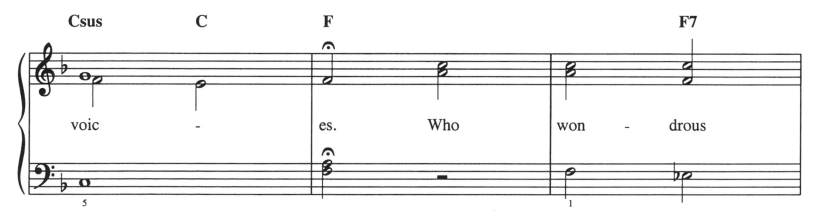

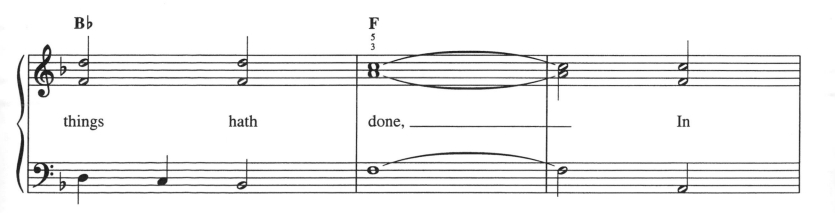

whom His world re - joic -

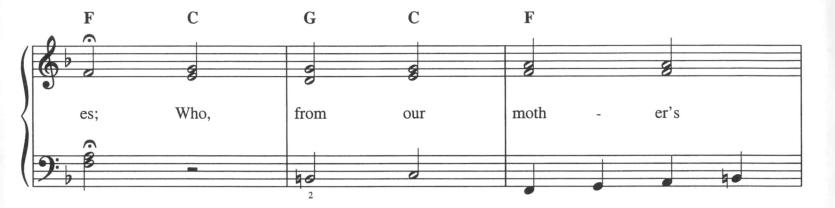

es; Who, from our moth - er's

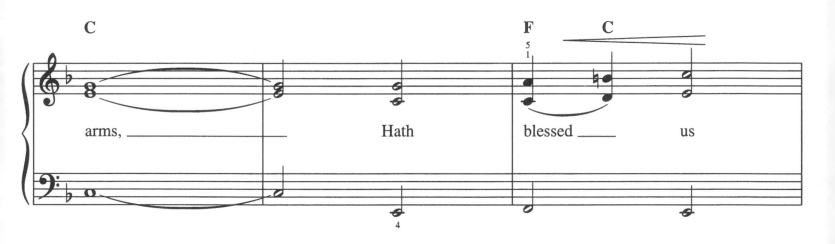

arms, _____ Hath blessed _____ us

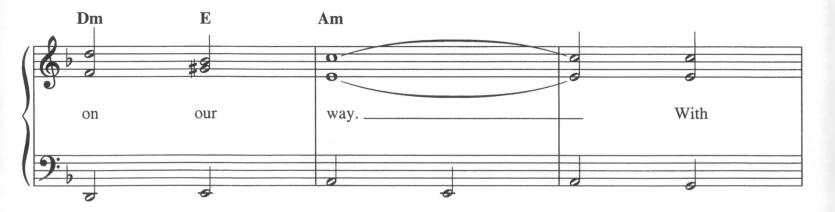

on our way. _____ With

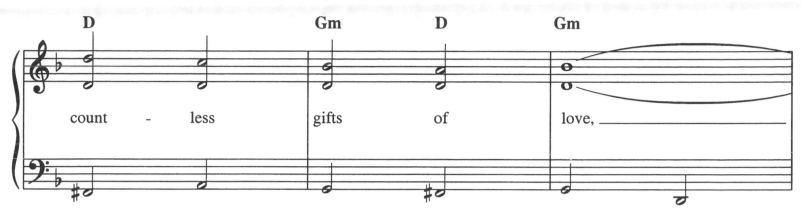

count - less | gifts of | love, ____

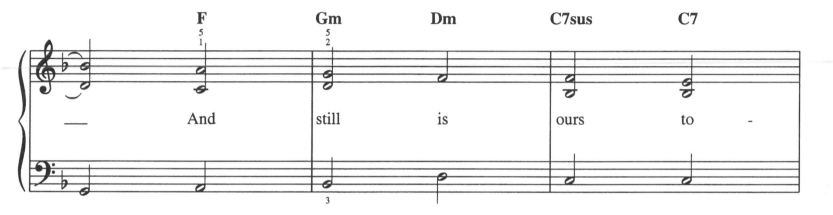

____ And | still is | ours to -

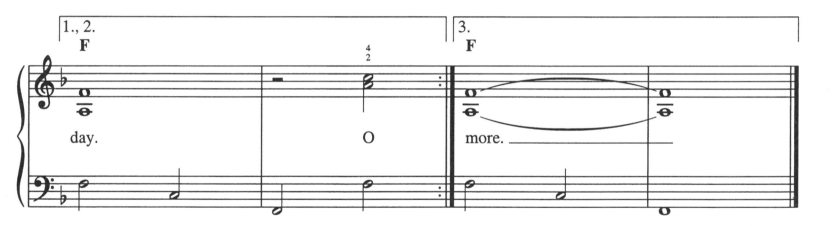

day. | O | more. ____

Additional Verses

2. (O) may this bounteous God through all our life be near us,
   With ever joyful hearts and blessed peace to cheer us;
   And keep us in His grace, and guide us when perplexed,
   And free us from all ills, in this world and the next.

3. (All) praise and thanks to God the Father now be given,
   The Son and Him who reigns with them in highest heaven;
   The one eternal God, whom earth and heav'n adore;
   For thus it was, is now, and shall be evermore.

A MIGHTY FORTRESS IS OUR GOD

Words and Music by MARTIN LUTHER
Translated by FREDERICK H. HEDGE

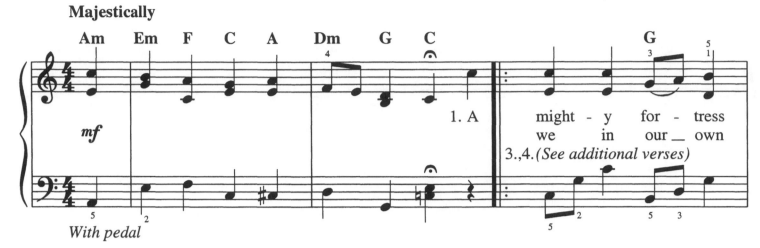

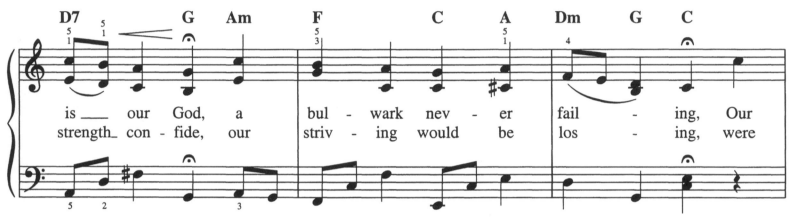

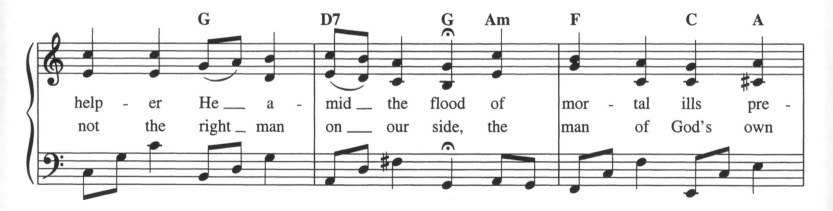

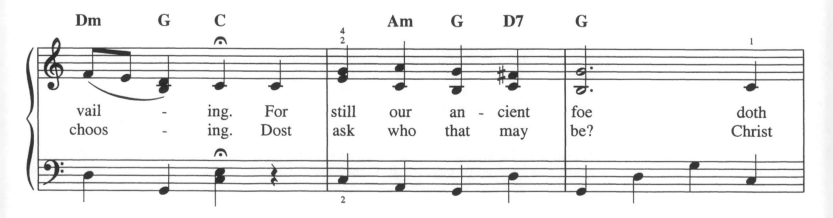

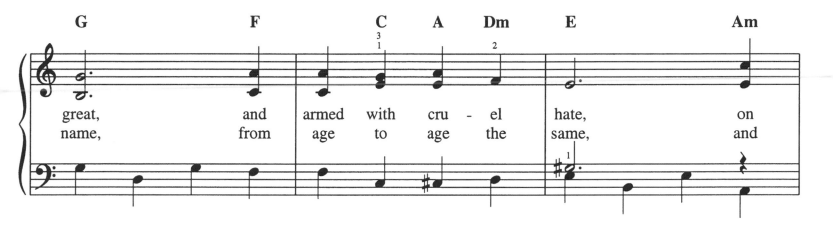

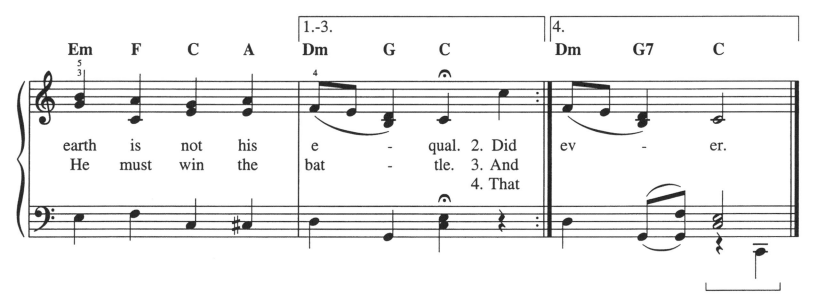

Additional Verses

3. And though this world, with devils filled,
should threaten to undo us,
we will not fear, for God hath willed
His truth to triumph through us.
The Prince of Darkness grim,
we tremble not for him;
his rage we can endure,
for lo, his doom is sure;
one little word shall fell him.

4. That word above all earthly powers,
no thanks to them, abideth.
The Spirit and the gifts are ours,
through Him who with us sideth.
Let goods and kindred go,
this mortal life also.
The body they may kill;
God's truth abideth still;
His kingdom is forever.

NEARER, MY GOD, TO THEE

Text by SARAH F. ADAMS
Music by LOWELL MASON

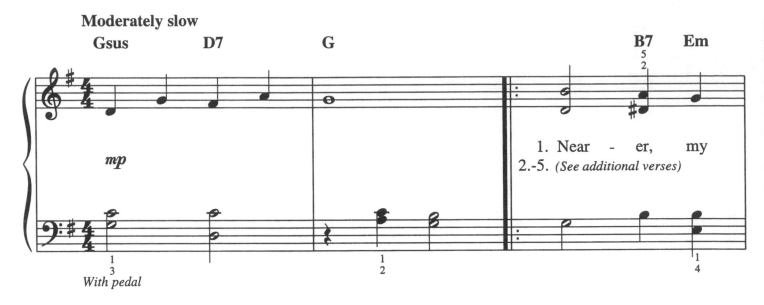

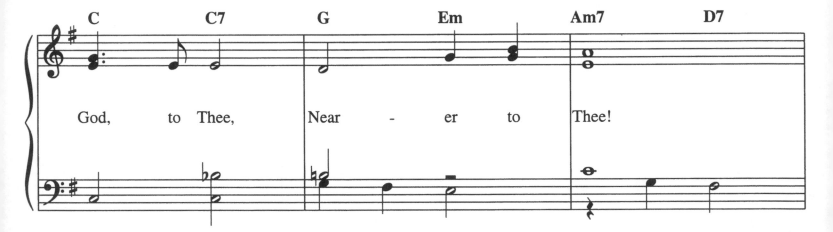

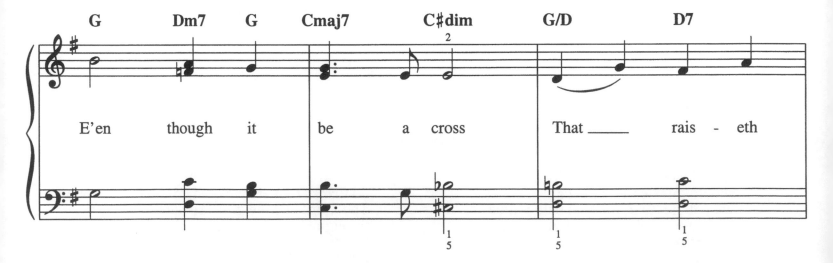

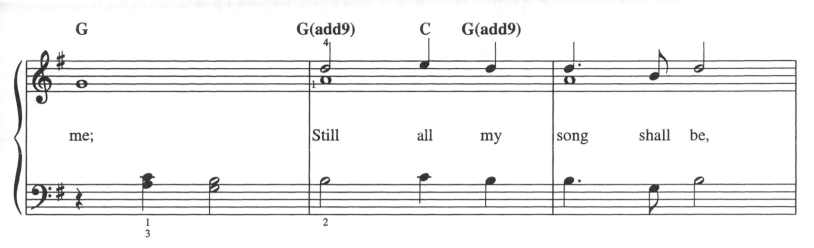

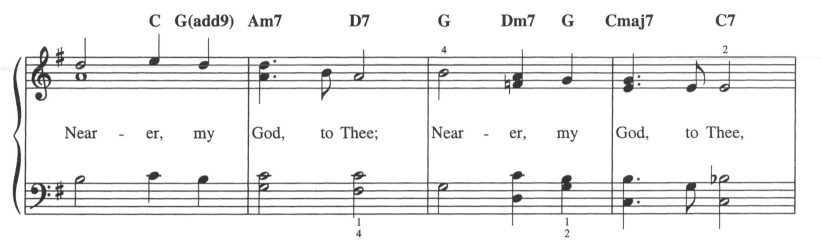

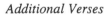

Additional Verses

2. Though like the wanderer,
   The sun gone down,
   Darkness be over me,
   My rest a stone;
   Yet in my dreams I'd be
   Nearer, my God, to Thee!

3. There let the way appear
   Steps unto heaven:
   All that Thou sendest me
   In mercy given:
   Angels to beckon me
   Nearer, my God, to Thee!

4. Then, with my waking thoughts
   Bright with Thy praise
   Out of my stony griefs
   Bethel I'll raise;
   So by my woes to be
   Nearer, my God, to Thee!

5. Or if on joyful wing
   Cleaving the sky,
   Sun, moon, and stars forgot,
   Upward I fly;
   Still all my song shall be,
   Nearer, my God, to Thee! Amen.

O FOR A THOUSAND TONGUES TO SING

Words by CHARLES WESLEY
Music by CARL G. GLÄSER
Arranged by LOWELL MASON

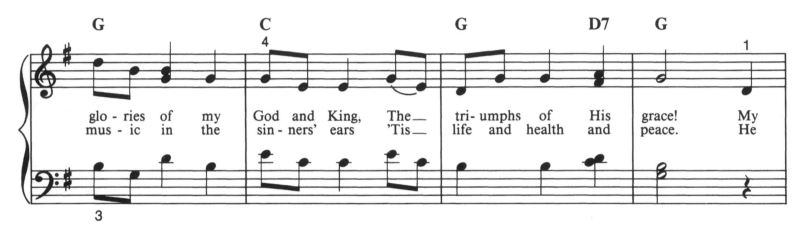

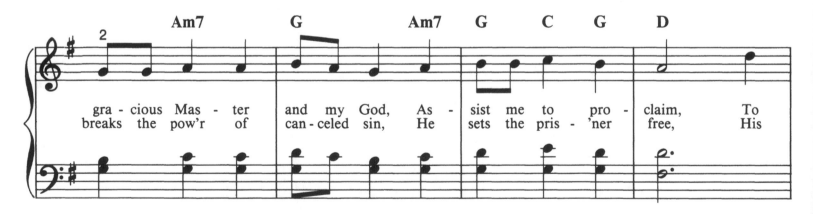

O GOD, OUR HELP IN AGES PAST

Words by ISAAC WATTS
Paraphrased from Psalm 90:1-5
Music by WILLIAM CROFT

THE OLD RUGGED CROSS

Words and Music by
REV. GEORGE BENNARD

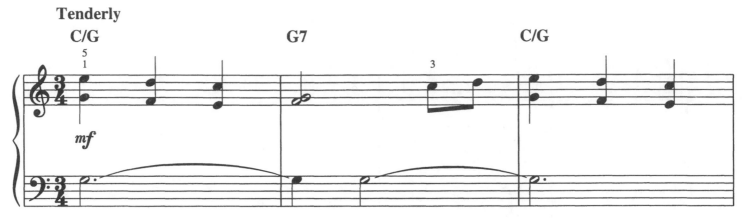

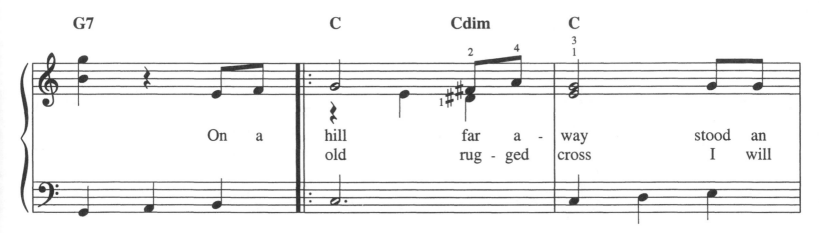

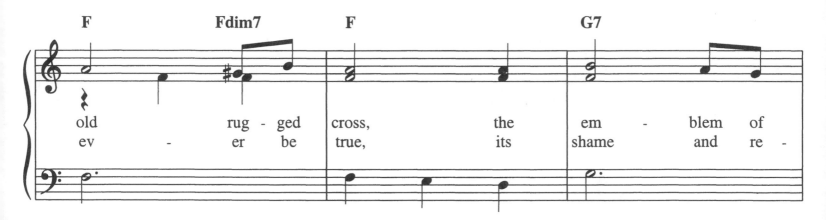

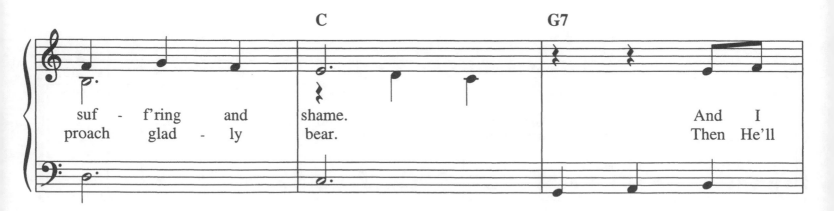

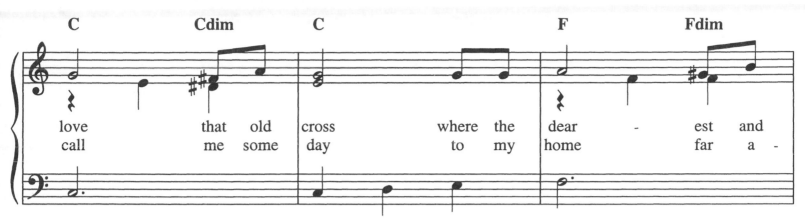

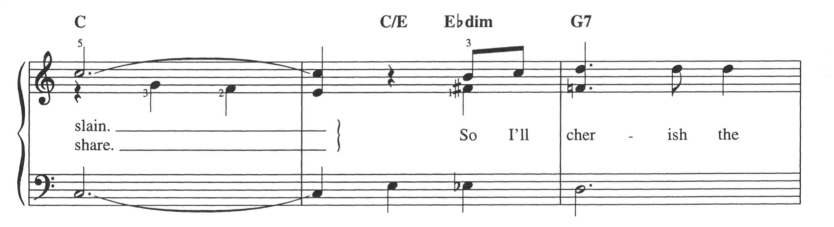

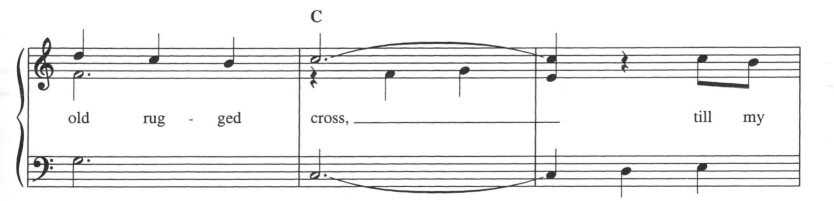

F　　　　　　　　**F♯dim**　　　　　　　　**G7**

tro - phies at　　last I lay　　down. _____

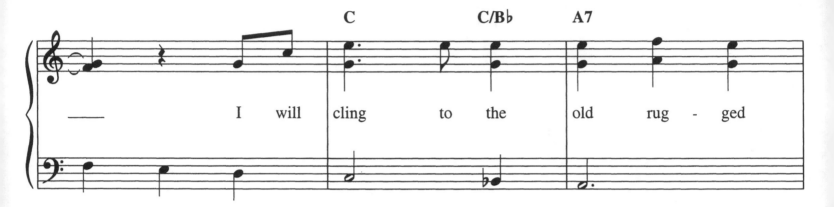

C　　　　**C/B♭**　　**A7**

_____ I will cling　　to the　　old rug - ged

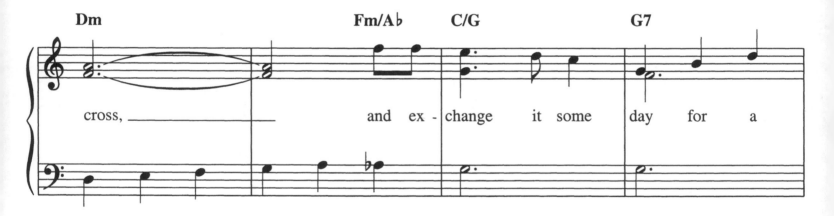

Dm　　　　　　　**Fm/A♭**　**C/G**　　　　**G7**

cross, _____　　and ex - change it some day for a

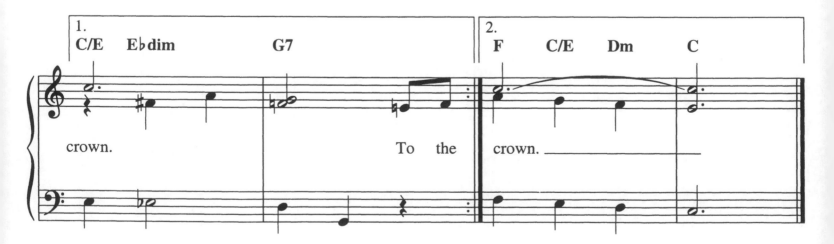

1.
C/E　**E♭dim**　　　　**G7**

2.
F　**C/E**　**Dm**　　**C**

crown.　　　　　　　To the | crown. _____

OPEN MY EYES, THAT I MAY SEE

Words and Music by
CLARA H. SCOTT

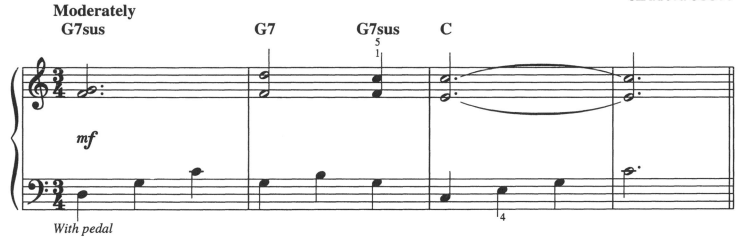

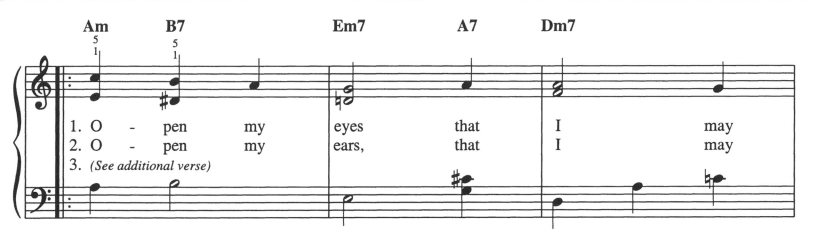

won - der - ful key
sounds in my ear,

That shall un -
Ev - ery - thing

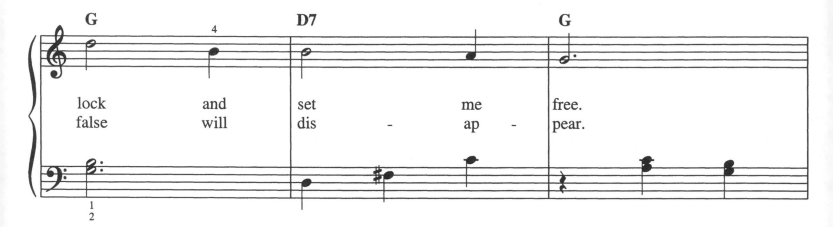

lock and set me free.
false and will dis - ap - pear.

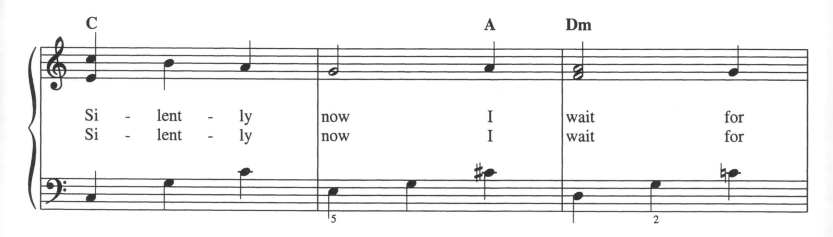

Si - lent - ly now I wait for
Si - lent - ly now I wait for

You, Read - y, my God, Your
You, Read - y, my God, Your

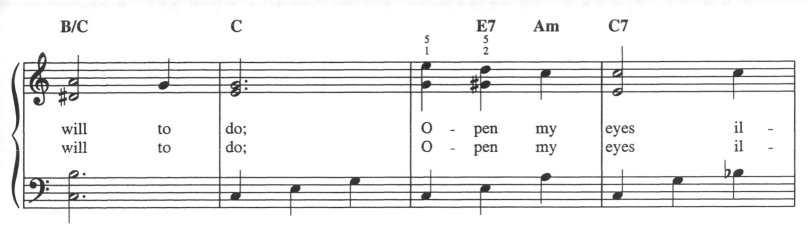

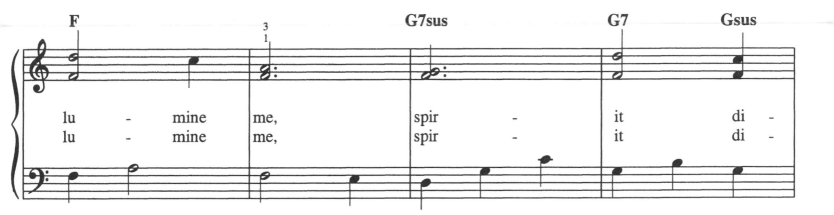

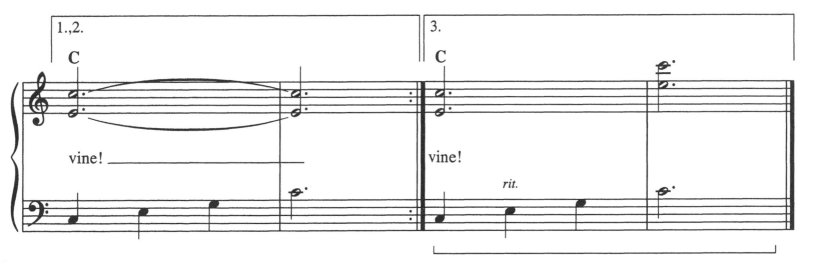

Additional Verse

3. Open my mouth, let me declare
   Words of assurance everywhere;
   Open my heart, and let me prepare
   Your loving kindnesses to share.
   Silently now I wait for You,
   Ready, my God, Your will to do:
   Open my heart, illumine me,
   Spirit divine!

ONWARD, CHRISTIAN SOLDIERS

Words by SABINE BARING-GOULD
Music by ARTHUR S. SULLIVAN

Like a slow march

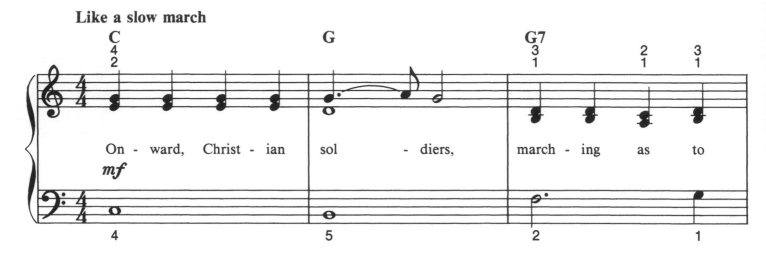

On - ward, Christ - ian sol - diers, march - ing as to

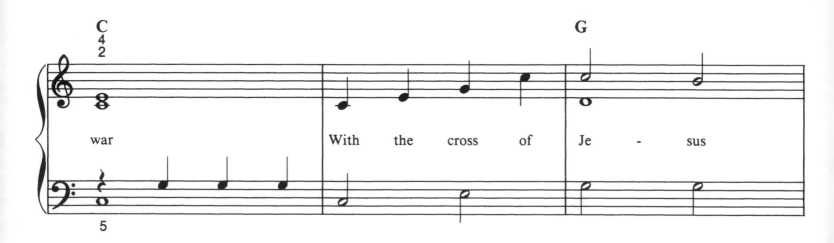

war   With the cross of Je - sus

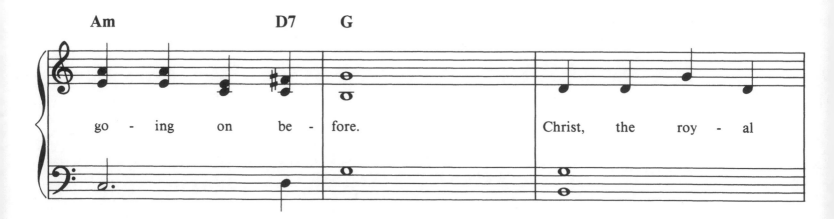

go - ing on be - fore.   Christ, the roy - al

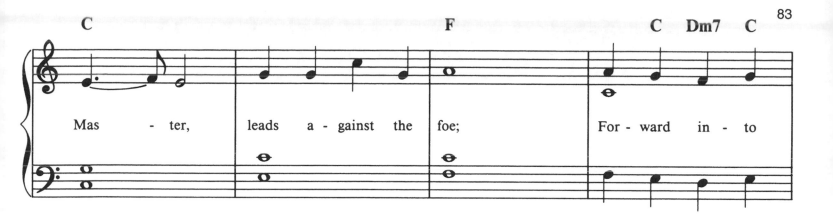

Mas - ter, leads a - gainst the foe; For - ward in - to

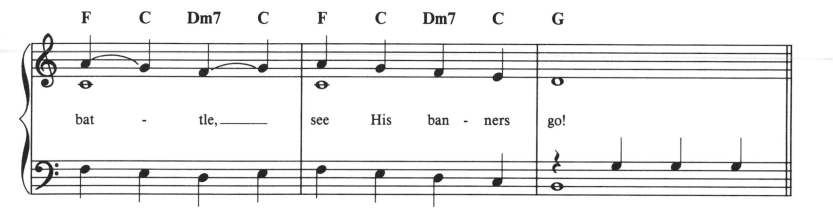

bat - tle, _____ see His ban - ners go!

On - ward, Christ - ian sol - diers, _____ march - ing as to _____ war,

f

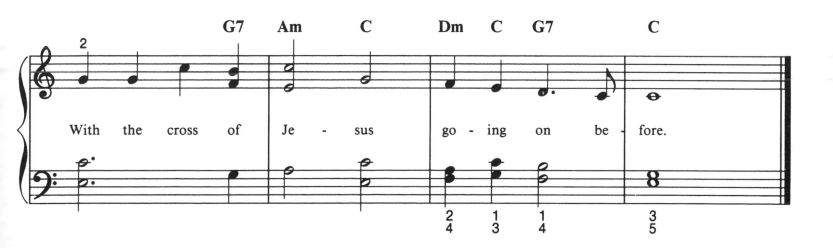

With the cross of Je - sus go - ing on be - fore.

PRAISE GOD, FROM WHOM ALL BLESSINGS FLOW

Words by THOMAS KEN
Music attributed to LOUIS BOURGEOIS

Moderately slow

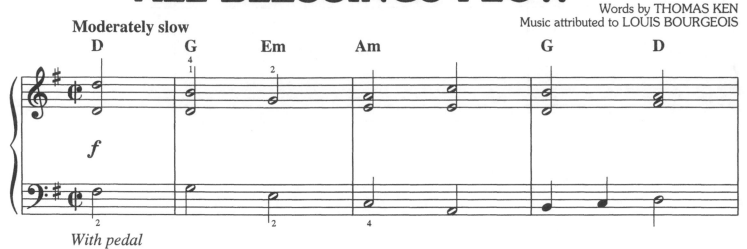

With pedal

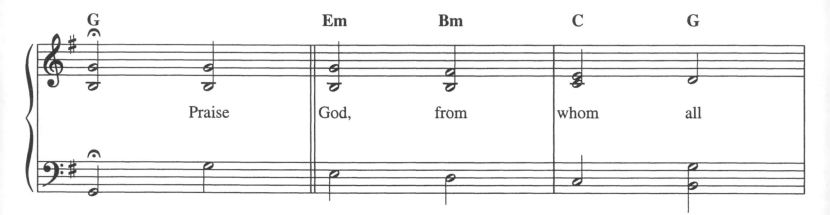

Praise God, from whom all

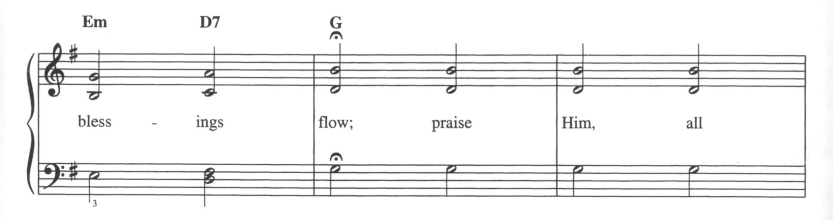

bless - ings flow; praise Him, all

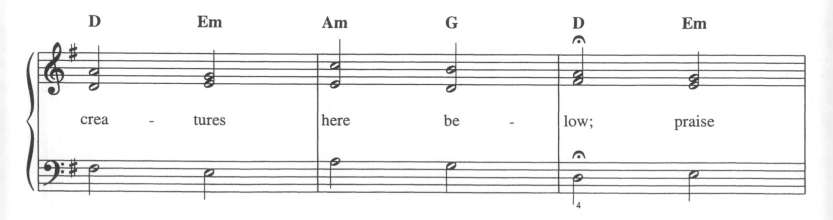

crea - tures here be - low; praise

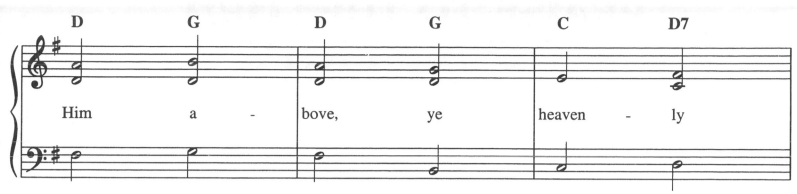

Him a - bove, ye heaven - ly

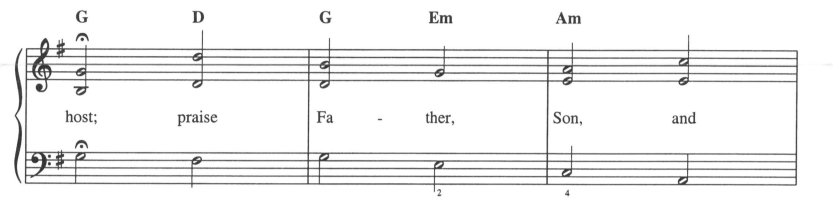

host; praise Fa - ther, Son, and

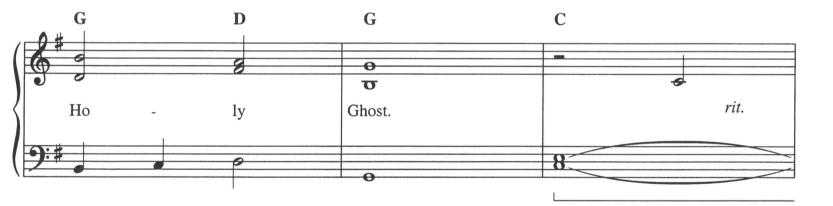

Ho - ly Ghost. *rit.*

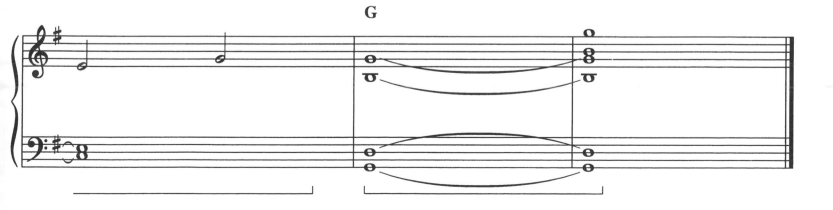

PRAISE TO THE LORD, THE ALMIGHTY

Words by JOACHIM NEANDER
Translated by CATHERINE WINKWORTH
Music from *Erneuerten Gesangbuch*

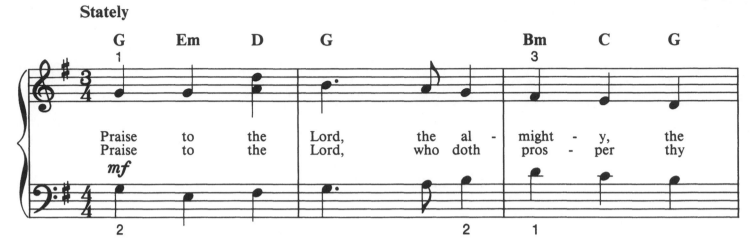

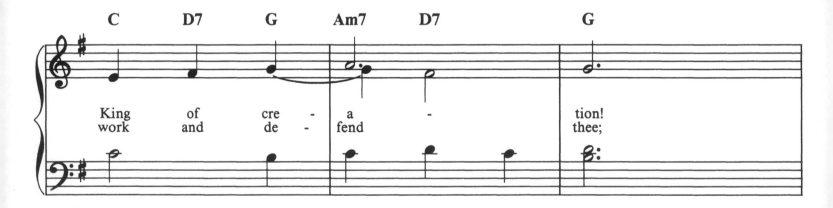

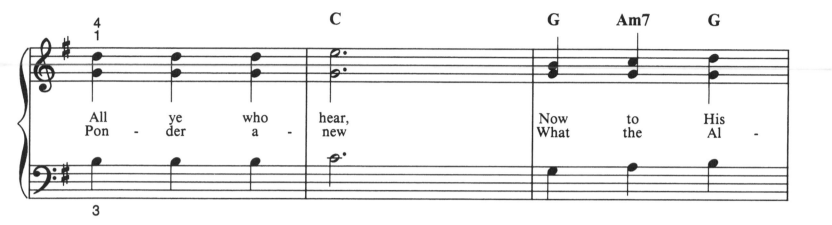

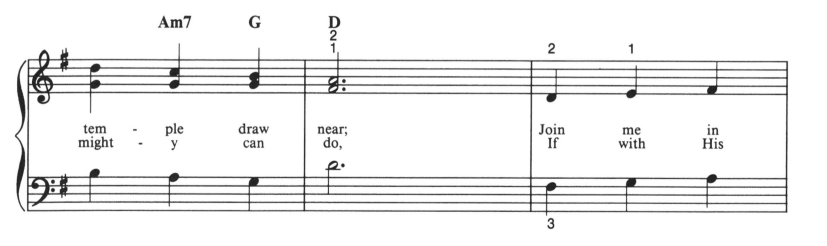

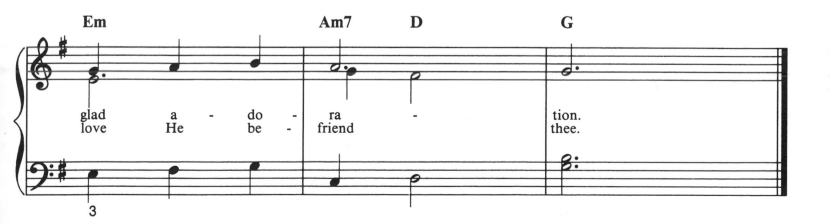

PRECIOUS MEMORIES

Words and Music by
J.B.F. WRIGHT

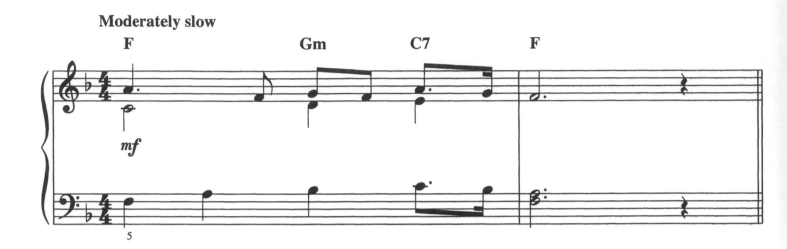

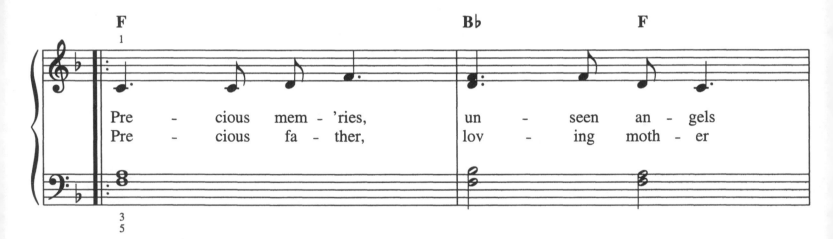

ev - er near me   And   the sa - cred past un - fold.
of   my child - hood   In   fond mem - o - ry   ap - pears.

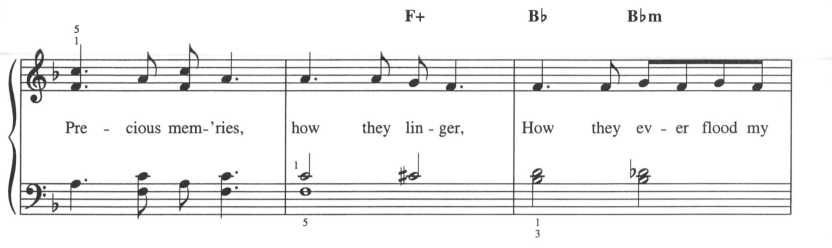

Pre - cious mem-'ries,   how   they lin - ger,   How   they ev - er flood my

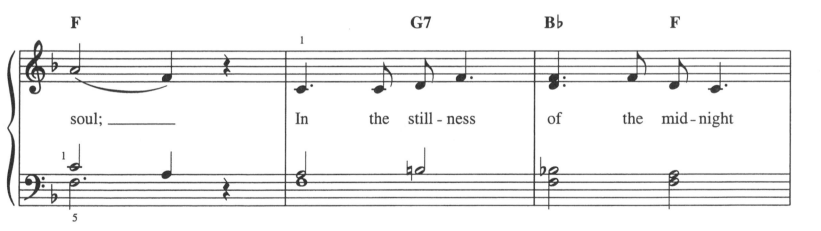

soul; _____   In   the still - ness   of   the mid - night

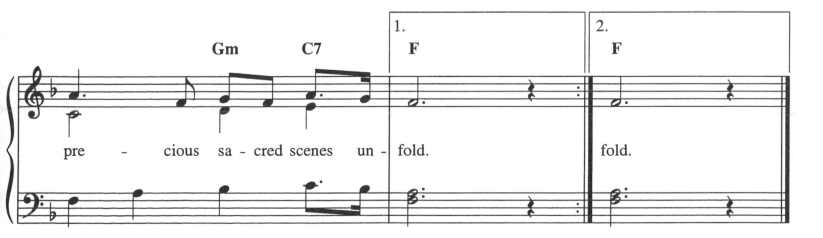

1.   2.

pre - cious sa - cred scenes un - fold.   fold.

ROCK OF AGES

Words by AUGUSTUS M. TOPLADY
Music by THOMAS HASTINGS

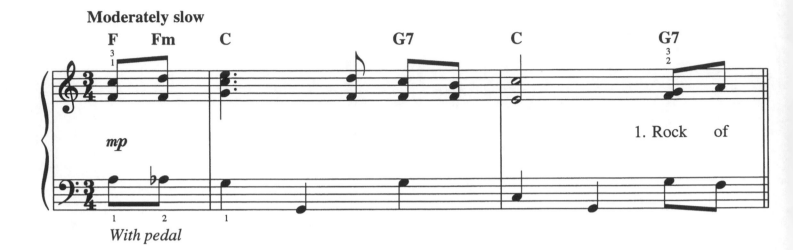

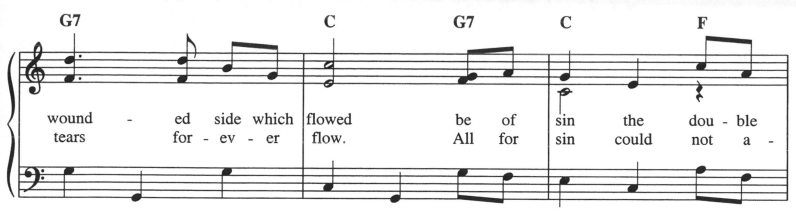

wound - ed side which flowed be of sin the dou - ble
tears for - ev - er flow. All for sin could not a -

cure; save from wrath and make me pure. Not the
tone; thou must save, and thou a - lone. Noth - ing

1.-3.

4.

thee. *rit.*

Additional Verses

3. Nothing in my hand I bring,
   simply to the cross I cling;
   naked, come to Thee for dress;
   helpless, look to Thee for grace.
   Foul, I to the fountain fly;
   wash me, Savior, or I die.

4. While I draw this fleeting breath,
   when mine eyes shall close in death.
   when I soar to worlds unknown,
   see Thee on Thy judgment throne.
   Rock of Ages, cleft for me,
   let me hide myself in Thee.

SOFTLY AND TENDERLY

Words and Music by
WILL L. THOMPSON

Moderately slow

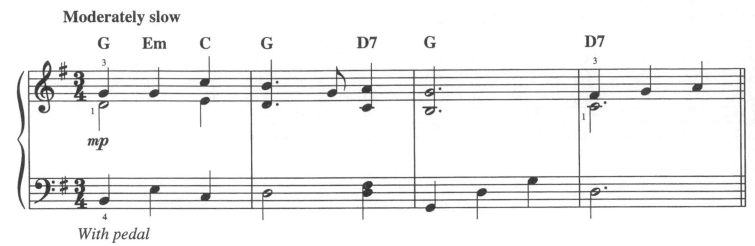

With pedal

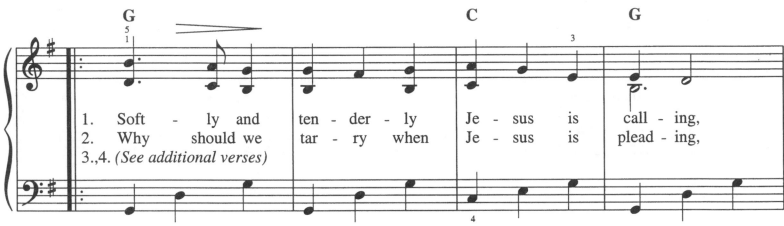

1. Soft - ly and ten - der - ly Je - sus is call - ing,
2. Why should we tar - ry when Je - sus is plead - ing,
3.,4. *(See additional verses)*

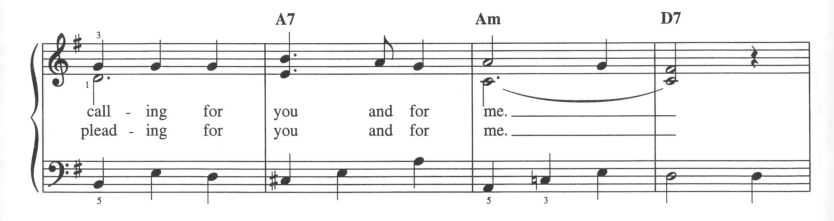

call - ing for you and for me. _____
plead - ing for you and for me. _____

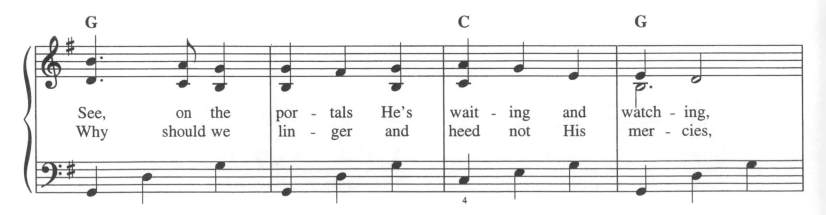

See, on the por - tals He's wait - ing and watch - ing,
Why should we lin - ger and heed not His mer - cies,

watch - ing for you and for me._____
watch - ing for you and for me?_____ Come

home,_____ come home,_____

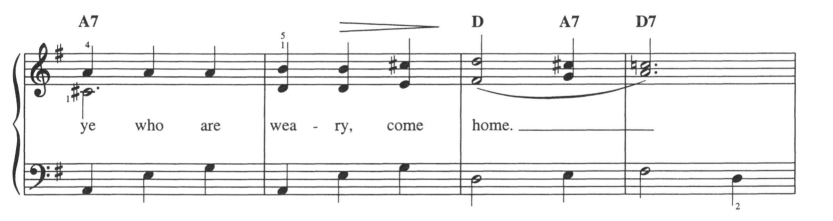

ye who are wea - ry, come home._____

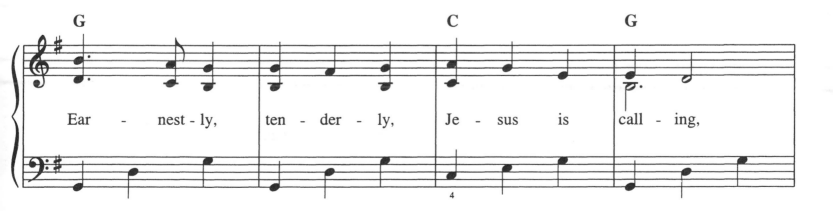

Ear - nest - ly, ten - der - ly, Je - sus is call - ing,

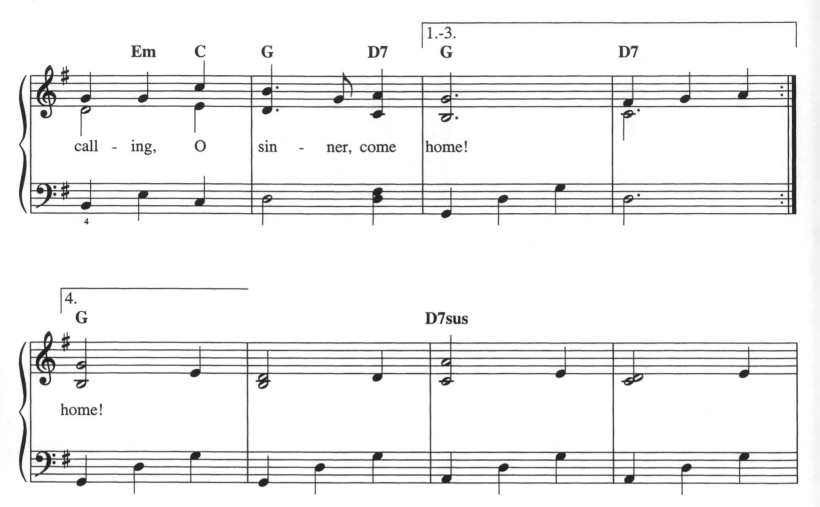

Additional Verses

3. Oh! for the wonderful love He has promised,
   promised for you and for me.
   Tho' we have sinned, He has mercy and pardon,
   pardon for you and for me.

4. Time is now fleeting, the moments are passing,
   passing for you and for me.
   Shadows are gathering, death beds are coming,
   coming for you and for me.

SWEET HOUR OF PRAYER

Words by WILLIAM W. WALFORD
Music by WILLIAM B. BRADBURY

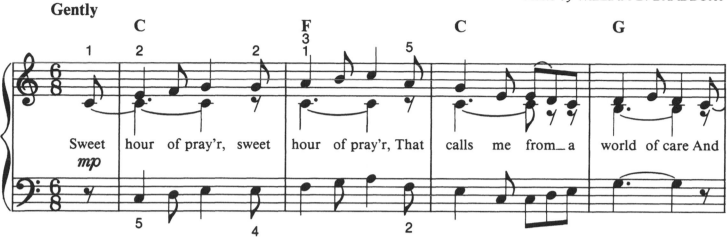

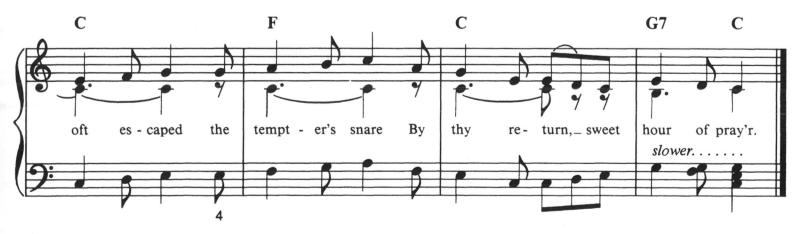

SWEET BY AND BY

Words by SANFORD FILLMORE BENNETT
Music by JOSEPH P. WEBSTER

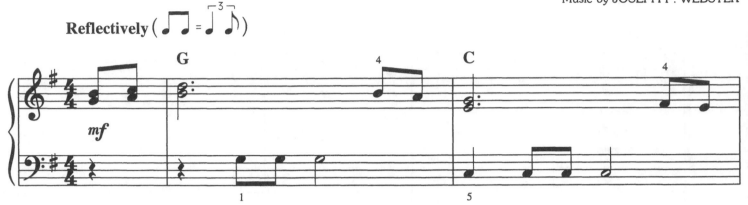

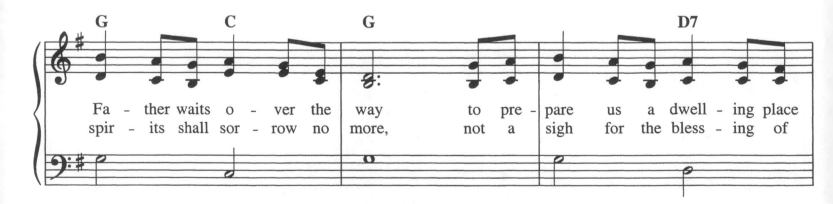

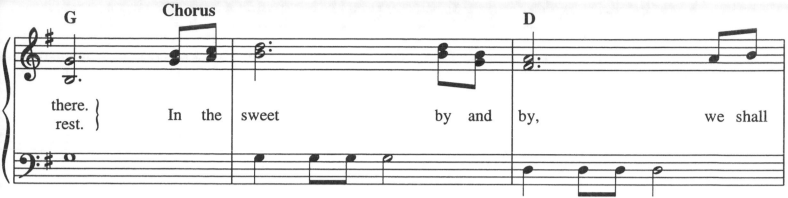

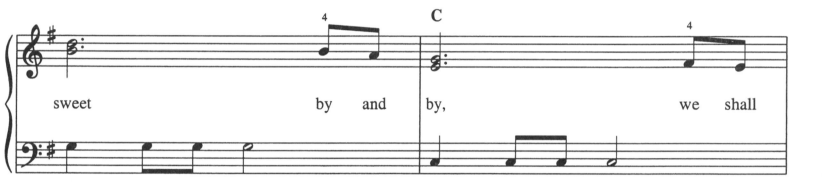

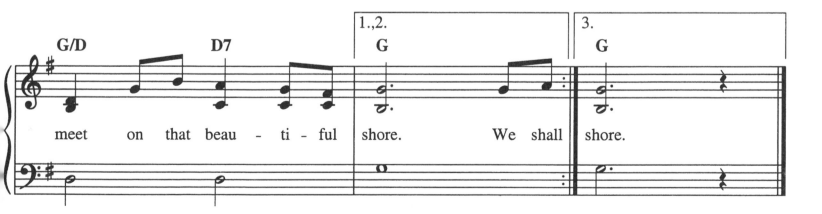

Additional Verse

3. To our bountiful Father above
We will offer our tribute of praise,
For the glorious gift of His love
And the blessings that hallow our days.
Chorus

TAKE MY LIFE AND LET IT BE

Words by FRANCES R. HAVERGAL
Music by LOUIS J.F. HÉROLD

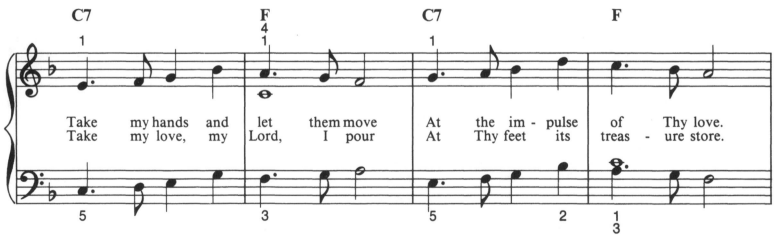

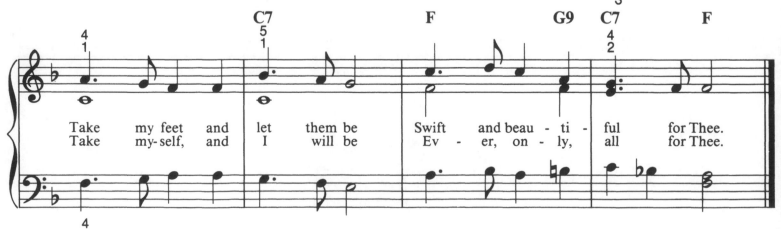

WE GATHER TOGETHER

Words from *Nederlandtsch Gedenckclanck*
Translated by THEODORE BAKER
Netherlands Folk Melody
Arranged by EDWARD KREMSER

Moderately, flowing

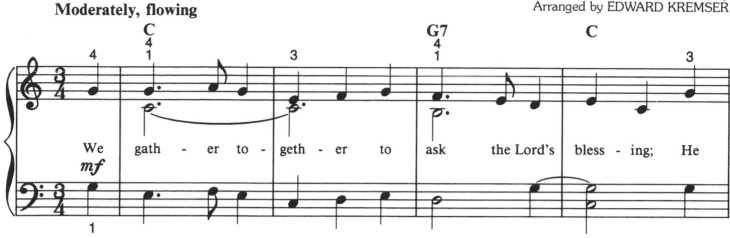

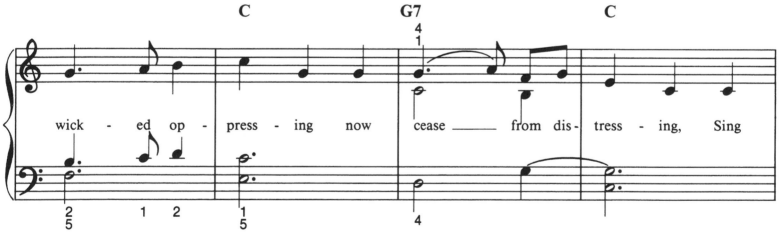

WHAT A FRIEND WE HAVE IN JESUS

Words by JOSEPH M. SCRIVEN
Music by CHARLES C. CONVERSE

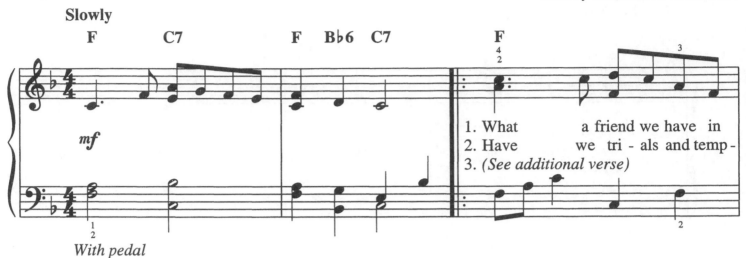

1. What a friend we have in
2. Have we tri - als and temp -
3. *(See additional verse)*

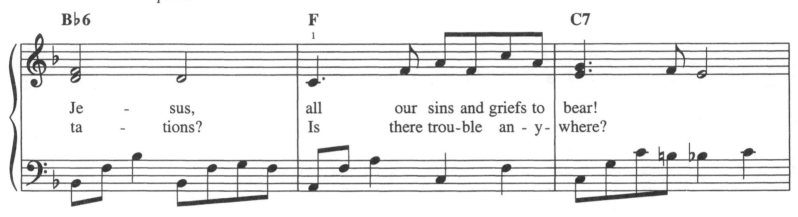

Je - sus, all our sins and griefs to bear!
ta - tions? Is there trou-ble an - y- where?

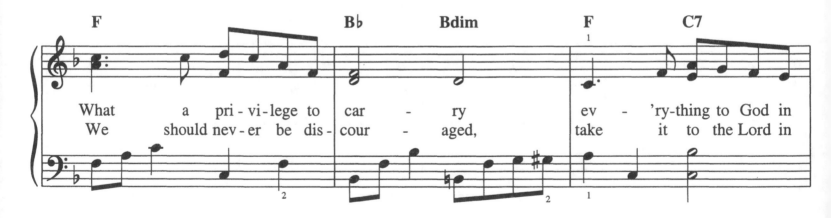

What a pri - vi-lege to car - ry ev - 'ry-thing to God in
We should nev - er be dis-cour - aged, take it to the Lord in

prayer! Oh, what peace we of - ten for - feit,
prayer! Can we find a friend so faith - ful,

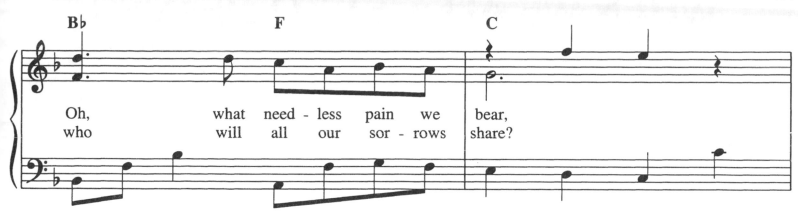

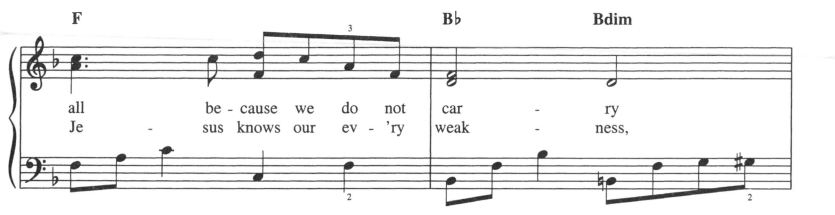

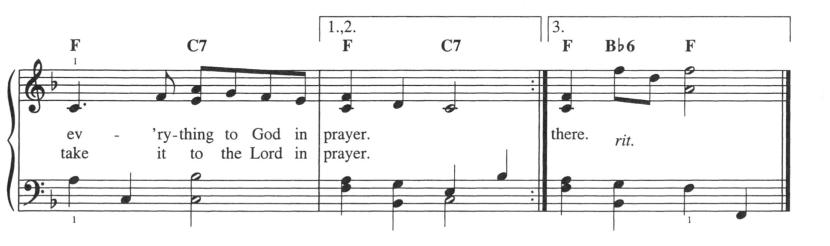

Additional Verse

3. Are we weak and heavy-laden,
   cumbered with a load of care?
   Precious Savior, still our refuge:
   take it to the Lord in prayer.
   Do thy friends despise, forsake thee?
   Take it to the Lord in prayer:
   In His arms He'll take and shield thee,
   thou wilt find a solace there.

WHEN WE ALL GET TO HEAVEN

Words by ELIZA E. HEWITT
Music by EMILY D. WILSON

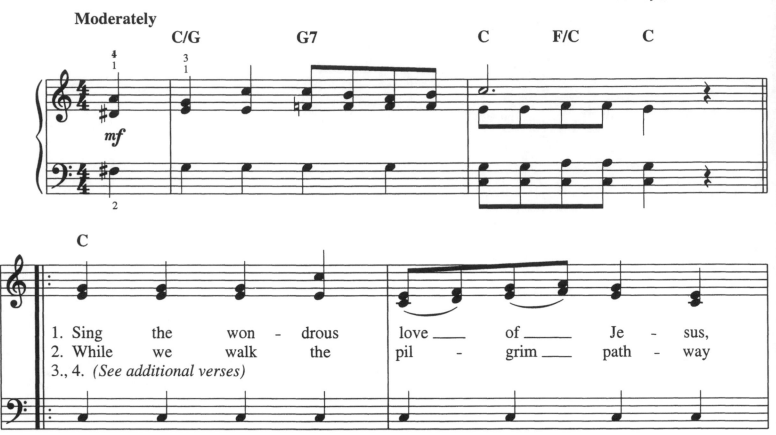

1. Sing the won - drous love ___ of ___ Je - sus,
2. While we walk the pil - grim ___ path - way
3., 4. *(See additional verses)*

sing His mer - cy ___ and His grace; in the man - sions
clouds will o - ver - spread the sky; but when trav - 'ling

bright and bless - ed He'll pre - pare for us a
days are o - ver, not a shad - ow, not a

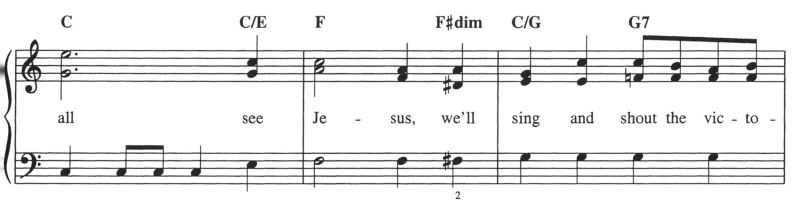

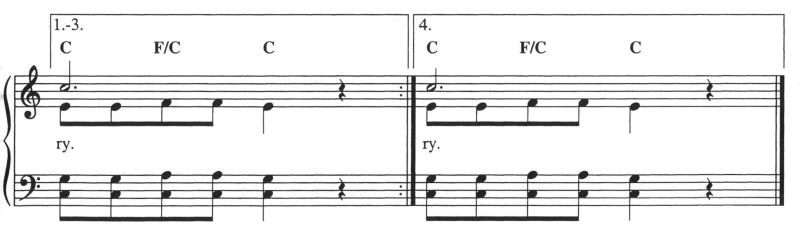

Additional Verses

3. Let us then be true and faithful,
   Trusting, serving every day;
   Just one glimpse of Him in glory
   Will the toils of life repay.
   Chorus

4. Onward to the prize before us!
   Soon His beauty we'll behold;
   Soon the pearly gates will open,
   We shall tread the streets of gold.
   Chorus

WHEN I SURVEY
THE WONDROUS CROSS

Words by ISAAC WATTS
Music arranged by LOWELL MASON
Based on Plainsong

With feeling

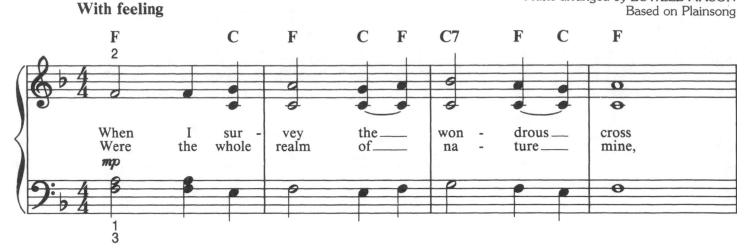

When I sur-vey the____ won - drous____ cross
Were I the whole realm of____ na - ture____ mine,

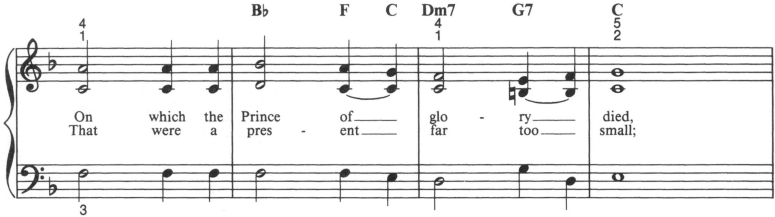

On which the Prince of____ glo - ry____ died,
That which were a pres - ent____ far too____ small;

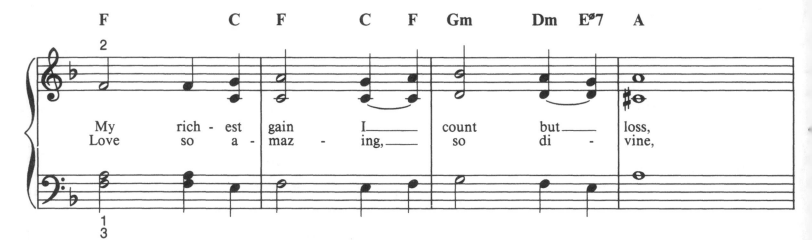

My rich-est gain I____ count but____ loss,
Love so a - maz - ing,____ so di - vine,

And pour con - tempt on all my____ pride.
De - mands my soul, my life, my____ all.